Paris Survival Guide
for Expatriates, Students,
Non-French People and Other
Curious Bystanders:
131 Ways to Make Your
Parisian Life Easier

Marianne Ly

DEDICATION

To my son Alex

Introduction

Bonjour, mes amis. I hope you are excited about going to Paris. You should be. Regardless of whether you are planning to move there or simply spend some time in the City of Light or go there for a brief visit or just dream about Paris, there is so much to discover.

If this is a new experience for you and you plan to stay for any length of time, it will be a change in lifestyle. You will be surrounded by people speaking a language that is not yours. You may feel a little lost, at least at first. It could be that nothing will be familiar to you, neither the people and their habits nor the city itself. For some people, it may be exciting and exhilarating. For others, it will be daunting. If you are in the second category of people, this book is for you, and even if you happen to be in the first category of people, you may learn something about spending time in Paris that you may not know about.

If you are an expatriate being assigned to Paris, like many business people I met over the years when I was an interpreter, translator and bilingual assistant, or if you are a student who is planning to spend a semester or two in this city, like I did (and ended up living there for 23 years), you may already have some idea of what your Parisian life is going to be like, but I'd like to share some of my own personal recommendations with you as well as a few anecdotes that I hope you will find helpful, interesting or amusing. Most guide books are going to give you ideas for visiting Paris but not always for living there. What I am going to share with you is about what to expect when you spend some time in this city. If you are French and living in Paris, you probably know everything I am going to talk about, but if you are one of these non-French people, you may learn something new. If you happen to be simply a curious bystander with no particular plans to live in the City of Light, you may want to know a little bit more about what is involved, just out of curiosity, of course.

Since technology is so amazing these days, I suggest that when you are reading this book, you go online and bring up some pictures of the places or topics I talk about. I have provided a list of topics to google for each of my suggestions at the end of this book. All you have to do is google whatever I have listed and you will be able to have access to pictures of the topic being discussed. If you are just a curious bystander, maybe without any real plans to go to Paris, here is your chance to see yourself in the city virtually. That's what I love about technology: you can go there without being there.

As an American who lived and studied and worked in Paris for 23 years, I have an idea of what you may be experiencing and I understand why living and staying in Paris, despite its beauty and great attraction, can actually be a frightening experience for some people. Since I was a teacher who taught French in American schools for twenty years, I know that learning a new language can sometimes be challenging. In addition to the language difficulties, any move involves major changes in your way of life, but moving to a foreign country is sometimes like going to another planet. But do not panic. Paris is one of the best planets to discover. Paris will grow on you and you will come to see the city and its inhabitants through totally different eyes.

All of the recommendations or suggestions I make for you in this book are based on my own personal experience and actual events. Like everything else, there are always exceptions to the rules, and when I tell you about French people and my impressions of living in Paris, these are my own personal opinions and views based on my own experience in this city. Times change and some things do change too, especially due to the pandemic that started in 2020, but Paris is still there, waiting for you to discover it. In the following pages, you will find a list of suggestions with some explanations, not necessarily in the order of importance or in any particular order, but I hope you enjoy reading about Paris and learning a little more about what it's like to actually live in this city that makes so many people dream.

| 1) | Learn the language and don't be afraid to speak out. |

Above all, learn the language and don't be afraid to talk to people around you *en français*, of course. It's undoubtedly the first biggest step to take, because you need to build confidence in yourself and your ability to communicate with the people around you.

I must warn you that you may once in a while come across a French person who will try out his English on you when you are trying out your French on him. You may say something in French to him and he may see that you are struggling or detect some type of accent, and he will pitch in and attempt to find a few English words to say back to you. Do not let this discourage you from trying out your French. Your French is probably much better than his English, so keep at it. Be brave, speak out, use French, and learn.

French is a beautiful language, which is why many people who are not French love to learn the language and listen to it. French pronunciation, however, can be difficult at first because of the various sounds that do not exist in your language. You have to learn to talk through your nose for nasals and swallow the r's that have nothing to do with English r's. You have a u that is somewhere between e and u in English, but with practice and a little (and maybe even a lot) of effort, you will manage and also progress.

You may be one of these people, like myself, who worries about his accent. I was very conscious of this when I started learning and I would occasionally become tongue-tied when talking with people I didn't know, and maybe that will happen to you too. There are, of course, some rare individuals who are very gifted for picking up accents and speaking languages like a native, but I have found that almost all of these people speak several languages or were brought up speaking different languages, and there aren't too many people like that.

Almost everybody has some sort of accent, so don't worry about it. It's part of the beauty of our world.

Don't let anyone intimidate you in your efforts to learn and speak French, and you may find yourself getting intimidated quite a bit in Paris. I myself managed to get beyond this first milestone when I went to classes at the Sorbonne years ago. I will always remember a stern and stout lady French professor who looked like she could have been an opera singer and who wore the same gray jacket and skirt every day of the year. She used to call out our names to read from a French book. "Lisez et lisez BIEN" (read and read well) is what she used to bark out in a booming voice that echoed throughout the classroom. "Lisez et lisez BIEN," she would repeat, as if there was something about that "bien" part that we all didn't understand. Everybody, of course, sat in the back of the classroom and tried to hide under the desks, but she always found somebody. However, as the year went by, I slowly became accustomed to this terror in the classroom and ended up saying to myself, "Yes, I will read and read VERY WELL." It probably was not the case in reality, but I had convinced myself that I could do it to my own satisfaction, and so can you.

I suggest that you speak whatever type of French you can with people you know, your neighbors, with students if you at a school, with a French girlfriend or a French boyfriend, with co-workers if you are working, with people in stores and cafés and restaurants. You will learn through your mistakes but only if you make an effort to speak the language. Little by little you will build vocabulary and use more new words than you ever realized you could. You will hear the language and eventually absorb the language.

Many years ago, language labs used to be very popular in schools and in colleges. You could practice saying different sentences after a native or near-native speaker or you could answer questions and then listen back to a recording which allowed you not only to learn phrases and vocabulary but also to compare your accent to the person who was talking without an accent. There are now apps online that you can find or software packages that you could use if you are worried about speaking French and concerned about your accent. It is a much more passive task to read and write French than to speak the language, but to communicate with people around you every day, you are going to have to speak. Like everything else, the more you practice, the better you get at it.

To be able to communicate, you will, of course, need to remember vocabulary and expressions. Years ago, I used a small notebook to write down any new words or expressions I had learned in day-to-day life. Writing down the words will help you remember them. I used these words every day, made some really ridiculous mistakes, but this is how you learn. Try it. You'll find yourself improving as each day goes by. This is learning through immersion, which is what you have the opportunity to do. You will hear so much French that you will eventually be thinking and dreaming in the language. It takes quite a while to reach this level, and to be fairly fluent in the language, it will probably take you about two years of being immersed, but it is worth all the effort you put in. Learning another language opens up a whole new world around you. This will be the new you.

If you have the chance to take classes to learn the language, there are many options. Some people I know have gone to Alliance Française which has excellent programs in many different cities, including Paris. Many colleges in the U.S. have excellent study abroad programs that will allow you to develop your language skills and discover the country at the same time, and even though the pandemic that started in 2020 has temporarily put a halt on some of these programs, they will most certainly start up again one day. Nowadays there are also many private tutors if you are looking for a few lessons and not a full course, and there are many courses online too that allow you to learn wherever you may be.

You can check out my own books if you want to review some French and understand some basic concepts behind the language. I have written two series of books to help you review and learn the language and hope to continue with others. My French Quiz Whiz books will give you a chance to test yourself and learn from any mistakes you may make since I provide detailed explanations in English in the key for each question. My French Fun books are vocabulary game books with 60 games in each book that you can play by yourself or with a classmate or friend. I wrote these books with college, high school and middle school students in mind, but even if you are an adult, you will find the basics you need. I wrote these books as supplements to different levels of courses you may be taking. If you are interested, check out my books at www.amazon.com/author/mariannely.

Years ago, I was enrolled in the program at the Sorbonne called Cours de civilisation française. This program is for foreign students only and includes not only language instruction but also classes on French politics, French philosophers, French literature and French history, just to name a few. This program has been around since 1919, so it is one of the most well-known programs you could enroll in. My French friends always used to joke around saying that the purpose of "les Cours de civilisation française" was all too obvious: "civiliser les étrangers," to civilize foreign students. Ha, ha, très drôle, I would tell them. I am sure that you will come to appreciate French humor, just as I did. I found that a lot of French people are witty and have a sharp sense of humor, and it is undoubtedly in France that I learned to laugh and to not take life so seriously. Maybe that will happen to you too.

Learning a language will open your doors to new experiences. Life becomes an adventure when you're learning another language, so go out and have fun with it.

2)	Get used to being watched by people sitting in cafés.

Parisians have a favorite pastime: people-watching. The city is full of cafés, and cafés are where many French people spend their spare time. It is the place where you take the time to get to know your friends or acquaintances. Generally French people like to meet their friends in cafés and not at home. Consequently, you will spend hours sitting at a table on the sidewalk or facing the street inside the café and seeing people in the street. People walking in the street are like people walking across a stage to them. They watch and observe and sometimes make a comment or two about what is happening in the street. You will find yourself doing the same thing eventually.

You have a wide choice of cafés in Paris, from the oldest and most renowned in the Latin Quarter and on boulevard Montparnasse to the local corner café where everyone in the neighborhood goes. The better-known cafés tend to be pricier than the others, and if you are more concerned about your budget, because cafés can be a costly habit if you go to the ones that are very well known, you have others that are less expensive in the Latin Quarter, which is where many college students go, or in other areas that are more residential, such as the 14ème arrondissement or the 15ème arrondissement. If money is a problem for you, you can order the cheapest item in a café, which is, of course, a small cup of black coffee, or have your coffee at the café counter which is less expensive because you have to stand and not sit down to get a discount. Coffee is the cheapest item in a café and if you decide to find a chair and table, you can sit for hours and be entertained by people-watching for as long as you want, just like the French do.

3)	Get rid of those sneakers

Times and styles may have changed, but you are still in the fashion capital of the world. Unless you want the people around you to think that you are a professional athlete, get rid of the sneakers and try some shoes that are more like city shoes. A colleague of mine once went to Paris and made the mistake of wearing her sneakers. A French man came up to her and asked if she was planning to go and play tennis. My poor colleague was confused and didn't know what to think of it. Why would he think she wanted to play tennis? Well, look at the shoes.

I am not telling you to put on some uncomfortable but stylish footwear, even though it is what some people do. The French say, "Il faut souffrir pour être belle." You have to suffer to be beautiful. Unless you want to be labeled right away as a foreigner, get something that looks like what most people are wearing.

The same applies to clothing. Most French people will not wear shorts in a city. If they are on a beach or in the country on vacation, it's different. In Paris, a lot of people are going to work and dress professionally. Dark colored clothing, especially black, is always in style in this city. Flashy clothes will make you stand out. If you want to stand out, fine, go ahead, but there will probably be people looking at you and wondering where you got your get-up or what strange country you come from.

While you're at it, get rid of that beret too even though I have heard that it has become a trend of some kind. It used to be that only old men playing pétanque (which is like bocce ball) in public squares walked around in those things. Thinking that all the French wear berets is like thinking that all Americans walk around in cowboy hats. Maybe some Americans do, but not all of them and certainly not everywhere in the U.S.

4)	Order coffee in a café, but don't drink too much.

Coffee in France is very potent stuff. That's why they give you such small cups. If you think you need more than one or maybe two, expect not to be able to sleep at all at night.

When I first arrived in France, I went to a café and was delighted to try the coffee. A small, white porcelain cup was placed in front of me on a tiny saucer. Did I need a lump or two of sugar? Sure. The cup was nice and warm and the coffee was delicious. I thought to myself, what a small cup. I'll have some more. I actually had three more, and believe me, I didn't sleep for two days. After that, my coffee was limited to one cup, early in the morning and one cup after lunch and that was it. You can always order decaffeinated coffee if you like to drink coffee all day, but you may find that the taste is not the same.

The French usually drink coffee at breakfast and after a meal. If you order coffee to go with your French meal, they will think something is wrong with you. Coffee is supposed to be consumed after you have finished a meal.

You will find there are different types of coffee you can order. You can have the small demi-tasse after a meal that is generally drunk black. If you ask for cream for this after-the-meal coffee, they will probably think you are weird or they will just say to themselves that you don't know any better because you are not French. You can have a café au lait or a café crème which is served in a larger cup and is coffee with milk or with cream. This is what most people have only around breakfast time. All the coffee served is much stronger than American coffee which French friends of mine so vividly call "jus de chaussettes" which literally means juice derived from soaked dirty socks.

5)	Don't use "tu" too freely.

One of the hardest notions for English-speaking people to get used to is this notion of the formal "you" - "vous" - reserved for everybody you don't know or don't know very well, and the familiar, fuzzy warm "you"- "tu" - that you may be tempted to use because it does seem friendlier and cozier than that cold, reserved, heartless, formal "vous." Keep in mind that you have to take time to go from "vous" to "tu" and in some cases, even after years, you will never reach the "tu" stage with certain people. Even in school, after seeing my students everyday out of the year, sometimes for two, three or even four years, I still had to remind my students that no, I was not their mother or grandmother and no, they were not supposed to use "tu" when talking to me, their teacher, even though I could use "tu" with them, basically because they were still young and it is permissible to say "tu" to a young person. "Vous" applies to teachers even if you see them all the time, because regardless of whatever profound love you may have for your teachers, your teachers are still not family unless you decide to officially adopt them. Use "vous" please.

If you are a business person, be particularly careful, because people get insulted if you talk down to them and saying "tu" to someone you do not know will not be well received. Students, on the other hand, tend to be more casual, but most of the time, you still start out with "vous" unless the person you are talking to says "tu" to you or asks if you would like to "tutoyer." Use "vous" for almost everybody and you won't go wrong. "Vous" is a polite form of you, and "tu" is used only for family members, very close friends, relatively young people, small children and animals. No, you are not going to say "vous" to your dog unless you treat him like royalty. If the person you are talking to doesn't fall into these categories, DO NOT USE TU.

Avoid by all means saying "tu" to sales people in stores

or your waiters in restaurants and cafés. You may risk getting your food thrown at you if you use "tu" when talking to a waiter, because he will think you are insulting him and treating him like an inferior being and not the respectable person he is. Do not say "tu" to your concierge either - the person who is the guardian of wherever you may be living if you choose to live in an apartment: if you do let "tu" slip out, you may never see your mail again.

French Canadians tend to use "tu" more freely than people from France. Remember that you are in Paris, not in Canada. I met a French man who organized stays for students in France a few years ago, and after spending 23 years in France, I was shocked when he used "tu" right away to talk to all the teachers who had brought students to Paris. I assume that he thought he was dealing with easy-going Americans who didn't know better and who used "tu" like Canadians did. He should have known better. I realized I had developed this sense of "vous" vs. "tu" over the years, because I didn't like the way I was being talked to. It was a lack of respect and a statement that he thought we teachers were ignorant, or else it was ignorance on his part, assuming we were the same as French Canadians. He should have offered to say "tu" instead of blurting it right out from the start, and you should do the same if you are not sure of where you stand with a French person.

6)	Meet your friends in a café.

Don't expect invitations to homes until you have known someone for years, and even then, you may never see their home. Homes are like sanctuaries to most Parisians and reserved for family and only the best of friends. Most people in Paris like to meet you elsewhere, in a café or a restaurant.

When I was a student, students used to go out in groups together, to restaurants, to movies, to cafés. I don't know if this has changed over the years, but it was something that was very different from what was generally done in the U.S. If you thought you were going to be one-on-one with somebody going somewhere, the next thing you knew, there were ten people tagging along.

If you are a student and know a French student, you may get invited to their home because you are both students, so you may get to know your friend's family and actually see where they live because of your common status as a student. If you are not a student, stick to the cafés.

I have always loved a very popular French TV program called "Plus belle la vie" and watched it for years, because it reminded me so much of the atmosphere and way of life in France. All the events in this soap opera take place at a café and you have a whole string of stories about the people going in and out of the café. Even though the story takes place in the southern city of Marseille, I found this particular program typical of life in France. If you have the chance to see it, check it out.

7)	Eat like a European.

You can generally tell where a person is from by the way he eats. French people usually hold the knife in their right hand and a fork turned upside down in their left hand. They will cut their food and eat directly without laying down the silverware. Americans will cut their meat, put the knife down, change hands and then pop whatever they cut into their mouth – a process that is much too long for the average French person. French people also keep both hands visible on the table, even if they happen to put their silverware down. Most of the time it is to break the French bread that goes along with every meal or to have a sip of water or wine that is usually served during a meal. French people may also find it peculiar if you put your left hand under the table since this is not part of their table etiquette.

8)	Learn to sleep on odd-shaped pillows called traversin.

These pillows are long and round and lie across the width of the bed. They are actually very comfortable, especially if you sleep on your side, but you do not find the likes of this pillow anywhere in the U.S. Most of the ones I have ever seen are stuffed with feathers.

I remember discovering these pillows years ago, when I was a student and staying for the first time in a student dorm and hostel called the Foyer International on boulevard St. Michel in the Latin Quarter, not far from the Luxembourg Gardens. I shared a small room overlooking the street with a French student. This dorm, which is for women students only, was built in 1928 and is a beautiful reflection of what architecture used to be, with its wood paneling and floors, old ornate two-person elevator and library and study rooms. If you are a young woman planning to study in Paris, this is a wonderful place to stay. The study rooms and library are open to both men and women, so if you have the chance, go and check it out. This is where I studied and started out my long stay in Paris. This is where I first saw this strange pillow called a traversin lying on the single bed I was going to be using for the year.

9)	Get in the habit of eating bread like the French do.

There is always "une boulangerie" nearby and the French typically have bread with all their meals. In a restaurant, you will not be served bread right away, like they do in the U.S. Bread was made in France to absorb all those wonderful sauces they pour over their delicious

dishes. Bread will be served at the start of the first part
of the meal, l'entrée, which is the appetizer, then with the
main dish and of course with your salad and cheese. Do
not ask for butter for the bread either. The only times you
will find butter on French bread is if you go to a café and
order a sandwich that would have butter on it, such as
"un sandwich jambon beurre" – a ham sandwich with
butter, or if you are having breakfast and are eating "une
tartine" – French bread and butter which is often
accompanied by jam too.

Don't expect a paper bag or a wrapper for your French
bread at the bakery either. The loaves are always lined up
along a wall and are fresh and sometimes even warm. The
baker will hand you your "baguette" with a little paper
around it. It's up to you to get it home safely.

You will see that there are many different kinds of
bread, but the most popular one is, of course, "la
baguette" which most people in the U.S. know as French
bread. If you are homesick and want the kind of loaves of
bread you find in the U.S., you can go to a supermarket
and look for "pain de mie." You will not, however, find
peanut butter anywhere around to put on your "pain de
mie" since peanut butter is not popular with the French.
You would have to go online to order your "beurre de
cacahuètes."

10)	Change some of your money before you go to France.

You may want to change some of your dollars into
euros before you head to France, so that you at least have
some cash on hand. How long you will be staying will
determine how you are going to take care of your money
situation. The exchange rate varies from day to day, but
generally stays around approximately the same value. If
you have a credit card, many of them can be used and
your bank will take care of making the calculation and

the conversion, but you may not get the best exchange rate because of banking fees. You have to be very careful that nobody pickpockets your wallet if you are carrying cash, but if you do have cash, you have currency exchange offices that will buy your dollars and sell you euros at good exchange rates. You can also use traveler's checks which is safer, because if they are stolen, you can get them replaced, but you still have to keep the paper with the check numbers in a safe place, separate from the checks. If you are staying for a longer period of time or if you are going to be receiving funds from a French company or organization, you will need to set up a bank account at one of the major French banks in Paris.

11)	Open a French bank account.

If you are going to be in Paris for a longer term, it would be best to open a bank account in a French bank. You will, however, need to become a resident first and obtain the appropriate permit for your stay. There are a number of banks you could use. A few of the largest and most used ones are BNP (Banque nationale de Paris), Société Générale and Crédit Agricole. You can contact them directly to find out their requirements for opening a bank account, but generally you need to show them your resident permit, proof of where you are living (by showing a utility bill) and some proof of employment or income.

If you want to use a savings bank, Caisse d'Epargne is the most popular one. They add interest to your account at the end of the year, and if you plan to buy a home in Paris or anywhere else in France, they offer mortgages with low interest rates.

The post office even offers banking services and in recent years, has expanded the types of services it offers.

If you are working, you can arrange for direct deposits – un "virement" – into these accounts. Having an account also allows you to easily deposit any checks you may have and to have access to a bank for all your financial needs.

12)	Watch out at ATM machines.

Keep in mind that you are in a major city, even though you may sometimes have the impression of being in a large village in Paris. Thefts are common in the city, and when entering your password at an ATM machine, be sure that nobody is looking over your shoulder to get the code. Watch your wallet too, after you get your money.

If your card gets stuck in the machine for some reason, take your cell phone out immediately and contact your bank, and do not let the machine out of your sight. I worked in a company years ago and had a colleague who lost his card in one of the machines. He left the machine and when he came back, both his card and all his money were gone. His account was covered for theft, so he eventually got the stolen money back, but it was a complicated process.

13)	Get ready to celebrate holidays differently.

The French have many more holidays with working days off than in the U.S. Some holidays are similar to the one in the U.S., such as New Year's Day, Christmas, and Easter, but others are different. Usually Easter Monday in France is a day off from work, whereas in the U.S., it is often Good Friday. Do not send greeting cards for Christmas until after Christmas, typically to wish friend a happy New Year, and you have until the end of January to send out your cards.

Special dishes are prepared for Christmas and it is one of the rare times a French person would eat turkey, because turkey is not a common food found in France. For Christmas, an elaborate meal called "le Réveillon" is usually prepared, and many people attend midnight masses in their local churches on Christmas Eve. A special cake called "la bûche de Noël" which looks like a yule log is prepared for the occasion. French kids do not have stockings for Santa, they leave out their shoes for "le Père Noël" and hope that "le Père Fouettard" does not come around with his whip to find children that were naughty.

"La fête des rois" on January 6 celebrates the arrival of the three magi, and it is not a day off from work since it is celebrated on the first Sunday of January. A special delicious pastry called "la galette des rois" is sold in pastry shops for the occasion. A small token, made out of either porcelain or plastic, depending on the price of your galette and where you buy it, is placed inside the galette and the person who has the slice with the token wins "la couronne" – a golden paper crown that is provided with the pastry.

You may think that in the City of Love, you are going to celebrate Valentine's Day, but the French do not celebrate this day. There are usually no exchanges of flowers or cards or chocolates. C'est la vie.

You are not going to see any decorations or cards for St. Patrick's Day either, probably because there is not a large Irish population in France.

You may think that Mardi gras is going to be fun in Paris too, but it is not. For most French people, it is a religious day marking the beginning of Lent with Ash Wednesday on the following day. There are some cities in southern France that may have festivities for it, but you won't find any in Paris.

April Fools, called "Poisson d'avril" in France, is not an official holiday, but it is very popular, especially among young people and children who love to sneak around and tape a paper fish on your back.

Easter in France has chocolate crosses and chocolate bells rather than chocolate rabbits as is the tradition in the U.S. You will have to look high and low to find jelly beans anywhere – jelly beans are not French.

Pentecost, a religious holiday, is no longer given to workers as a day off since a few years ago, the government asked people to continue working this day to support aid to senior citizens who had been suffering and dying from heat waves that had hit Paris. Paris is not equipped with air conditioning, unless you happen to be in one of the more modern or more luxurious hotels or modern offices.

May 1st is Labor Day in France and a flower called "le muguet" (lily of the valley) is found everywhere to celebrate the occasion. Many, many years ago, everything in France used to be closed on this day – there was no TV, no transportation, no restaurants, no movie theaters, no museums. It was almost like the prelude to "le confinement" (lockdown). However, in recent years, changes have come about and even though stores may not be open, you still have many places to enjoy.

May 8th is a holiday to commemorate V-Day in France, marking the end of World War II. Usually there is a ceremony at the Arch of Triumph this day.

What we call Bastille Day is on July 14. Do not expect to see a parade with floats or clowns or fictitious characters in costumes. All the parades you see in Paris are military ones. Even with "le confinement" in 2020, there was still a ceremony that was televised and the different branches of the military and their military equipment were all present, even if spectators on the street were not. Jets flew above the Champs-Elysées and left blue, white and red streams of smoke representing the French flag, just as they have done for decades now for this national holiday.

August 15, Assomption, is another religious holiday and therefore many people have this day off.

The French decided they liked the idea of having some fun before All Saints' Day and the Day of the Dead, so they adopted Halloween a few years ago. Children will dress up in costumes for parties, but there is no Trick or Treating. Until the 1990's, this was never celebrated.

November 1st is All Saints' Day. Usually people

remember those who are no longer with us and go to cemeteries with flowers. Many years ago, I went to the American Cemetery in Normandy for this day. There were over 9,000 American soldier who lost their lives on D-Day during World War II, and each grave is marked by a white cross in this cemetery by the ocean.

November 8 is a holiday to commemorate the end of World War I. World War I and World War II had such huge impacts on life in France that they are still remembered in ceremonies today.

You are not going to find French people celebrating Thanksgiving because this is an American holiday. There are, however, some hotels that cater to American expatriates and offer special turkey dinners on that day.

14)	Get your dates straight.

For the French, the first day of the week is Monday (lundi) and the last day is Sunday (dimanche) since this is the order of the creation in the Bible. Every day on a French calendar bears the name of a saint. Until a few years ago, all French children had to be given a name that appears on the calendar, so you did not have the possibility to give your child some weird and unusual first name if the baby was born in France and registered there. A lot of people avoided this by using the middle name or a nickname if they preferred a name that was not on the official calendar. Many French people will celebrate their birthdays but also have a smaller celebration for the day of the saint for whom they have been named. You wish them "Bon anniversaire" for their birthday and "Bonne fête" for the saint's day.

Unlike in the U.S., dates are expressed in French with the day first and then the month. This means that when you are using only numbers, for example, 3/6/21 for a French person is June 3, 2021 and not March 6.

When you are writing out dates in French, you are

going to just put the number in front of the month. For example, April 5th would be written "le 5 avril." You are going to use cardinal numbers – just plain numbers, and not ordinal numbers, like first, second, third, etc., for dates in French. The exception to this rule is for the first day of the month, which can be written out (such as "le premier avril") or put in an ordinal number (1er avril).

When you write letters, you are always going to indicate where you are writing from along with the date. For example, you'll have "Paris, le 20 février 2021" on your letter written on that date.

| 15) | Be extra polite with people you don't know. |

Add "monsieur" and "madame" or "mademoiselle" to people you don't know. "Merci, monsieur" and "Merci, madame" or "Merci, mademoiselle" are handy expressions to use. You can say "Excusez-moi de vous déranger" (sorry to disturb you). Say simply "pardon" if you bump into someone or need to say you're sorry for some reason. When you walk into a small specialty shop such as a bakery or a pastry shop or a "pork shop" (une charcuterie), you will generally greet everyone in the store by saying, "Messieurs, Dames." (Gentlemen, Ladies).

If you are a business person, you will need to learn special expressions to begin and close your letter, and even if you are writing an email, there are still formal formulae to use. You will never add the first or last name of the person you are writing to, if you are writing a business letter or message. You will only use "Monsieur" or "Madame" to start your letter, and if you have contacted these people, you may even write "Cher monsieur" or "Chère madame" but you will not be adding last names. There are also certain ways to close the letter or email, so you will need to ask your French colleagues to give you some advice if you do not know how to do this or the expressions to use.

Most French people value politeness and they expect to be treated in the same polite way. One of the worst insults you can say to a French person is that he is "mal élevé" – poorly brought up. Even from a very young age, children learn the importance of being polite and respecting the people around them.

16)	Be a person, not any employee.

The Parisians and other French people in general that you meet will talk to you as a person and will not identify themselves with their jobs, like many people do in the U.S. They will not talk about how much money they earn or what they have or what they do for a living. They do not have the same work ethic that many Americans have. They are more geared to leisure time, to their family and their own lives and personal interests when they are not at work. The people I knew were all professionals and had jobs, but the job stayed at the place of the job in most instances.

There are even stringent laws as to what an employer can or cannot do outside of working hours. Until recently, there were even laws against eating your lunch at your desk at your office and working at the same time, but with the "pandémie," it appears that some of these restrictions may be changing. Even though I had many French colleagues who had very busy jobs when they were on the job, I never heard the word "workaholic" in Paris. Maybe it doesn't even exist in French vocabulary.

17)	Don't expect to tour a French friend's house.

If, by chance, you happen to be invited into a French home, you will not be given the tour of the house, which is something many Americans like to do. Most French families feel that their homes are private, for them alone,

and you may see their dining room and their kitchen, but
not much more of their homes. Most Parisians live in old
apartments but the few houses in Paris or the others in
Parisian suburbs are always surrounded by a wall, which
is another indication of a desire for privacy. In the U.S.,
in most cases, when you walk outside to your lawn, you
may see your next-door neighbor and even start up a
conversation. Not so in France.

| 18) | Offer appropriate gifts if invited to a home. |

Flowers tend to be the gift with which you can't go
wrong if you are one day invited to a French person's
home. Boxes of candy or chocolates are sometime offered,
but they are not the first choice among the French for
gifts. Do not bring wine. Some French people are very
picky about what they drink and believe me, they know
their wines, and unlike in the U.S. where wine is a
popular gift to offer, it is not the same case in France. On
top of that, many times your French friends will have their
own supply of preferred wine that they keep in the
basement of buildings, in the storage area called "la cave."

| 19) | Learn to eat your meals in the proper order. |

Meals in restaurants and in homes are as symmetrical
as French architecture and gardens. You will start with
an "entrée" – no this is not the "entrée" we talk about in
the U.S. because in the U.S., it is a main dish. An "entrée"
in a French meal is the appetizer and it usually consists
of a soup or chopped vegetables called "des crudités" or
salami or pâté or cut-up tomatoes with oil and vinegar or
even radishes with butter. Once you have finished your
"entrée," you will be served the "plat principal" – the main
dish which is usually accompanied by some type of
vegetable. Then you will have your "salade" – usually a

salad made of lettuce and a light dressing of oil and vinegar. After that, you will have a choice of cheeses – le fromage – or else yogurt. After that, you will have a dessert which could be some type of pastry or pudding – la mousse – or fruit, which is also very popular when it comes to desserts. After dessert, you can drink your coffee and if you like alcohol, you can even have a pousse-café, a small shot of alcohol, to finish your meal.

In many restaurants, you can order a traditional meal for a price that includes everything and that is lower than what you would pay if you were ordering your courses separately. This is called "le menu" and you pay the "prix fixe." You usually can choose between two or three dishes for each course. In some restaurants, you may have three courses, and in others you may have the traditional 5 or 7 course meals. Regardless of how many courses are offered, you will save money by choosing "le menu."

| 20) | Watch out for "fake friends" in French. |

If you want to see the menu in a restaurant, you are going to ask for "la carte." If you are ordering one of the set-price menus in a restaurant that may offer them, you are going to order "le menu." When you are ordering "le menu," you usually have only a couple of choices for the appetizer, the main dish and the dessert.

If you look at a menu and think you are going to have a nice, cool drink of lemonade when you see "limonade," you will not be getting the drink you thought you'd have. "Limonade" is a soda similar to Sprite or Seven-Up. If you want to quench your thirst with lemonade, you need to order "un citron pressé" – a squeezed lemon.

"Cidre" on a menu is not just plain cider either. It's the hard liquor type of cider that you'll be getting.

Don't think that when you see "librairie," you are going to find a library. For a library, you will need to look for "la bibliothèque." Une librairie is a book store where you can usually buy school supplies as well. You usually find books, postcards, paper, school supplies, magazines and newspapers at the librairie.

Don't invent French either. Look up the words. It's easy to do these days. Some words in English may sound like words that could be French, but they are not. Please note that "garbage" is not French, nor is "jacket." When you're talking about garbage, you are going to talk about "des ordures" which doesn't even look like the English word. You can add a little French accent to "jacket" if you want, but to have a French person understand what you are talking about, you have to refer to it as "un blouson."

Be sure to keep your languages straight too. "Apartment" in English has one "p" but "appartement" in French has two and an "e" in the middle. You are "comfortable" in English but "confortable" in French. If you are going to wear a tuxedo, you are going to be wearing "un smoking" in French. You are going to park your car in "le parking" in French. As you learn, you will find out that there are quite a few words that look alike but either do not have the same meaning or have a difference in spelling.

My students always used to look at French words and think of English words, which is not what you should ever be doing, but they would do it just the same. Some of the boys would be embarrassed to talk about "arms" in French (des bras), because they were still thinking in English and not in French. The all-time favorite that some of boys in particular would ask me about was how to say "a seal" in French, like the animal you find in the ocean. The French word is pronounced like the F-word in English, so they would wait with great anticipation for the foul word they expected to have come out of my mouth, and I would always disappoint them with "une otarie" – another word for a seal in French.

21)	Be prepared to spend hours at the dinner table.

If you happen to be invited to someone's home for a special occasion or a holiday dinner, be sure not to make plans for anything afterwards, because in most cases, you will be spending hours at the table and eating and talking and talking and eating.

You will, of course, go through the different courses of a typical meal, but sometimes extra courses for the main dish will be added in. I myself recall attending a Bastille Day dinner with a group of French people at a Club Méditerranée resort in Switzerland many years ago. It was a fourteen-course meal that must have lasted at least three hours. In the middle of the meal, everyone was given a shot of alcohol, un pousse-café, to help us digest and continue eating. It was a good thing we were all at a sports resort with all kinds of activities to try to wear off some of that food. The food itself was wonderful, and in Paris, food in traditional restaurants is something that will help you survive any problem you may come across.

By the way, Club Med has changed ownership, but it still offers some unbelievable trips that are all inclusive. You pay one price that covers your transportation, your hotel at one of their many resorts throughout the world, all the activities you can do at these resorts, all the meals and even local tours that they organize.

22)	Wear your walking shoes during strikes.

Everything can shut down during a general strike and general strikes are not rare. Mail and deliveries come to a standstill. Even electricity will be cut off and transportation will come to a halt. Unions are very powerful in France. Even if you have a car, you will be stuck in traffic for hours because everyone had the same idea that you did and there is no other way to get to work or wherever you need to go, unless you have a motorcycle, which can be very dangerous to use in Paris since I knew a couple of people who had serious accidents with them. Parisians don't drive like most people in the U.S. Bikes might be the best way to go to wherever you need to go, but once you get to your destination, you probably won't be able to do much of anything unless you have charged up your laptop and can use it for hours. Otherwise, you might as well stay in bed or work remotely if that laptop allows you to do so.

I remember one general strike many years ago when I was working near the Arch of Triumph and living in the outskirts of the city, in a suburb called Puteaux. In the morning, I somehow made it in to the office that was located on Avenue Marceau which is around the corner from the Champs-Elysées, but since we all ended up sitting in the dark, and these were times before laptop computers and all these other technological marvels that exist today, we were all told to just go home. Of course, I had worn my most stylish high-heeled boots to the office. I ended up walking home, a three-hour hike past Neuilly-sur-Seine, across the bridge to La Défense and then all the way down to Puteaux. I had to soak my poor feet for hours.

| 23) | Learn to drive a car with a stick shift. |

Most Americans are used to driving a car that is automatic, but in Paris, if you do decide to have a car, you will mostly find ones with stick shifts. I myself did manage to find a Toyota that was automatic, but there was no power steering on it, so every time I went to turn or park, it was like driving a truck. That was the trade-off for being able to have an automatic car.

If you do have a stick shift car, you have to be very careful about rolling backwards on slopes and ramps with stoplights. There is a technique that I never mastered in gunning the engine and keeping the car going forward when you start moving. I had a stick shift car for about two months in Paris, many years ago, and I clearly recall having to put my emergency brake on when I was stopped on a slope, and the driver behind me ended up moving my car up to the street and a level area. I got rid of that stick shift car in no time, but maybe you will be better at driving in Paris than I was.

You can drive with your own license and your passport if you are spending a short time in France, normally less than 90 days, but you will, of course, need to get an international license if you are going to be staying for a while. If you will be spending more than a year in Paris, you can hand in your American driver's license in exchange for a French "permis de conduire." Unlike American licenses, the French licenses are valid forever.

The car you have may be smaller than the car you drive in the U.S. and you should be thankful for this small size, because finding a parking space in Paris can be difficult, and sometimes you have to squeeze the car into the tiny space. Don't be surprised to see cars trying to fit themselves into a spot by gently nudging the cars in front and in back of them in the parking spot.

You may, however, consider not having a car at all if you are in Paris, because unless you live in a building that has parking space, it is very hard to find spots on the street, and you could spend hours trying to find a place and end up spending just as much time walking to your home from wherever you can park the car. I don't recommend parking the car on the sidewalk, like some Parisians do. You could end up with a fine – un P.V. – or worse, they could put a clamp on your tire or haul it away completely, so you would have to go somewhere to pay what is due before getting your car back.

If you are inside the limits of Paris, you have all types of public transportation – the subway ("le metro") or buses or an express train system called the RER - to get you around without any problems. I myself lived without a car

for about 20 years and finally got one only because the
company I was working for moved out into the suburbs
and even though it was a fifteen-minute drive from my
home by car, it would have taken me over an hour and a
half to get there with public transportation.

If you really don't want to deal with a stick shift or even
a car, you could also take cabs or even rent a car
occasionally if you needed it. Most rentals, however, will
still be stick-shift cars.

One other solution would be simply to get out your
walking shoes and walk. I walked more in Paris than
anywhere else, but it is a great way to stay in shape and
also to see the city where there is always something
interesting going on.

24)	Learn the rules of the road if you dare to drive in Paris.

Not only will you need to know how to handle a stick
shift, especially on exits or ramps that have a slope, but
you will also need to get ahold of a booklet to become
familiar with the rules of the road, which are somewhat
different from what you will find in the U.S. For example,
if you are at a stoplight and want to turn left, and the car
facing you in the opposite direction also wants to turn
left, you are going to turn behind each other and not in
front of each other, like you do in the U.S. I had totally
forgotten about this when I came back to the U.S., and
my sister who was in the car with me was wondering what
on earth I was doing when I advanced into the
intersection and started turning behind the other car that
was also turning. After a while, it becomes second nature,
but you have to remember which country you are in.

Another difference to be aware of is for yielding, which
is the opposite of what it is in the U.S. In the U.S., the
right of way is given to the person on the left, so somebody
on a ramp has to let you pass by before they can come

onto the road. It is just the opposite in France, so if you are driving happily along, say on "le périphérique" which is a circular highway that goes around Paris, you have to let the person on your right – the driver that is coming down the ramp to get onto the highway – go in front of you.

When you are at stoplight, you cannot turn right when the light is red, as you can do in many states in the U.S.

Speed limits used to be much higher than in the U.S., especially when you got onto highways, but in recent years, there has been a movement to lower the speed limits to have limits closer to what we have in the U.S. On highways, you can still drive up to 130 kilometers an hour, which is about 80 miles per hour, but you will need to be outside Paris to be on roads with these speed limits. Recent changes in the speed limit in Paris have brought it down to 30 kilometers per hour or about 18.6 miles an hour, which, when you see how many cars and people there are in the streets of the city, is probably very reasonable.

If you happen to end up driving around the circle at the Arch of Triumph, the trick for getting around it is to let the drivers to your right coming into the circle go ahead of you. You do not need to keep up with the other drivers either. Most Parisians become speed demons when they get into that circle, but they have somehow developed a knack for weaving in and out of traffic without getting into accidents. You are not a Parisian. Take your time, even if some of those drivers around you start getting annoyed, and believe me, some of them will grumble and make gestures because road rage is very common in France and especially in Paris, but just ignore them.

My poor stepmother always refused to sit in the front seat of my little Toyota when I was driving in Paris. The first time she rode around the Arch of Triumph with me driving, she was clinging to her seat and turning a pale shade of white. After that, she just sat in the back seat, closed her eyes and prayed.

25)	Never tell a Parisian cab driver to go faster.

If you do take a cab, just sit back and let the cab driver do the driving, and hold on to your seat. There may be a speed limit in Paris, but most cab drivers totally ignore it. There are cab stations all over the city and most of the time, there is a line of cabs waiting to rush customers off to their destinations. If you need to go around the circle at the Arch of Triumph, they will weave in and out of traffic and take you down the Champs-Elysées in no time.

When you are at a stoplight, regardless of whether you are with a cab driver or with a Parisian who is driving, you will think you are at a starting block of some kind of race. Most French people who come to the U.S. always think Americans fall asleep at stoplights because it takes them so long to react and to move. It is totally the opposite in France, especially in Paris.

26)	Don't let French administrative red tape get to you.

Unless you are from a country in the European Union, you will need to have the appropriate papers to be able to stay for any length of time in France. The French administration just loves papers. They always seem to decide they need some paper that you never have with you, so you will end up making several trips to their offices to get your papers straightened out.

If you are a student, you will need to get a visa from the French consulate in the U.S. to be able to stay more than the three months allowed for tourists. If you are a business person, your employer will need to get a lawyer to handle your papers. In most cases, you will still need to go to your local Préfecture (police station) to register with the authorities. If you are staying for a year or two, you will need to get what is called "une carte de séjour" – a permit that allows you to stay in the country. Unless your employer or some organization takes care of this for you, you will need to stand in line, usually for hours, and show proof of your identity and normally some document that indicates you have a valid reason for being in France, such as employment that has been pre-approved by the French government or enrollment in a college. You will also need to show them that you actually live somewhere. If you are planning to work in France, your employer will need to arrange for you to obtain a work permit, "une carte de travail" because you cannot work in France if you do not have this permit. If you plan to live in France for several years, you will need to renew your "carte de séjour" for a few years every year until they finally decide to give you your "carte de résident" which is at first granted for five years and then can be obtained for another twenty, renewable every twenty years.

It is not unusual for police officers in Paris to check the identity of people in the street, so you need to have your papers and permits on you at all times.

If your children are born in France and if neither you nor your spouse are French citizens, you will need to register your child under your nationality, because unlike the U.S., being born in France does not automatically make you a French citizen. Any child of foreign parents has to apply for French nationality and go through naturalization procedures when they turn 18 if they want to stay in France and be French citizens.

| 27) | Sharpen your math and conversion skills. |

Math skills are definitely required if you plan to live in Paris and want to have at least some idea of how much money you are spending. Euros look like play money to people who are not used to paying with this currency, but if you sit down and start calculating prices in dollars, you may realize that this play money is vanishing too quickly.

At first, you will probably be confused by prices since

you will not be seeing dollar amounts in stores or supermarkets or in any place where anything is sold. Euros and the dollar equivalents fluctuate so you will need to consult the exchange rates in banks or online. If you take the approximate exchange rate in 2021, which is one euro is equal to 1.21 dollars, all you have to do to know how many dollars you are spending is to multiply the euro amount by 1.20. To make life easier, you can take ten percent of the euro amount and double that ten percent amount and add it on to the euro amount to know what it is in dollars. For example, if you want a pair of boots like a friend of mine had that cost 500 euros, you take ten percent of 500 which is fifty, double it, so you have one hundred and add it to the original cost of 500 and voilà, you have boots that cost 600 dollars, a real bargain for some stores in Paris.

If you have a certain amount of dollars and want to know how much you can spend in euros, you are going to take about 80 percent of the dollar amount.

Of course, you can always whip out your smartphone or pocket calculator and get an exact calculation for prices, but if you don't want to constantly have a phone or a calculator in your hand, these are just simple ways to have an idea of what you are paying.

When you go to buy food, you will, of course, be using the metric system and not pounds, so you will once again need to do some calculating to know how much meat or vegetables you are buying and what the prices are.

If you are conscious of your weight, you will be delighted to have it in kilos because it seems like less, but when you multiply it by 2.2 and find out how much you really weigh, you may decide to change some of your eating habits.

When talking about how tall you are, you will need to convert your measurements to centimeters. Clothing and shoe sizes will be different too, and the easiest way to find out your size is to try on clothes and shoes in a store or consult some size comparison charts online if you have access to a smartphone or a computer.

Temperatures will be in Celsius, so if they say it is 35° out, you are going to get your swimsuit out and not your winter coat. When you go to cook and are using a recipe, you will also need to use your conversion skills or consult a chart with equivalent values.

Speed limits are in kilometers, and you can calculate the miles by taking approximately two-thirds of the number in kilometers to find the miles. If you have miles, you will take half of the number in miles and add it to the number in miles to get the kilometers. After a while, all this math will become second-nature to you.

If you are looking for an apartment in Paris, you will not be talking in square feet like you do in the U.S. but rather square meters. You will soon realize that an apartment that is 60 square meters is not that big, even though it is the average size of an apartment in Paris. You will probably have a small kitchen, a living room, two bedrooms and a bathroom. C'est tout! (That's it).

28)	Learn to live without modern conveniences.

I once told an American business colleague that I never had a dishwasher (except for myself) during all the years I lived in and around Paris and he immediately declared that he would never be able to live in the City of Light. The more I think about it, I could not think of one single Parisian I knew who had a dishwasher either since most French kitchens are so old or so small that a dishwasher could never be installed. Some Americans can never do without everything that makes everyday living in the U.S. comfortable, such as being able to throw your dirty dishes into a dishwasher or drying your clothes in a dryer, which is another luxury item that most Parisian do not have, unless they happen to live in a more modern apartment building, which is not the case for most Parisians. Most of the time you will end up hanging your laundry in your bathroom, maybe on one of these racks that has a rope and a pulley so you can hoist it up towards the ceiling which is usually fairly high. It could be that you have a small room called "un séchoir" which is a little closet area reserved for hanging up laundry, but only more recent constructions seem to offer this type of space. You will not be allowed to hang any kind of laundry on your balcony because Parisians do not want to see any dangling clothes destroying the beauty of their surroundings. In some apartments, the laundry-hoisting contraption may be in the kitchen. Even your washing machine will be in your kitchen, because most apartments date back a couple hundred years, when none of these appliances were even dreamed of, and the kitchen has turned out to be the only part of a home where the pipes and water you need for your machine are located.

Air conditioning is another modern convenience that most buildings and homes in Paris do not have, unless you are in a more recent construction or a fancy hotel or modern offices, but it is still fairly rare. In any case, even though there may be a few very hot days in Paris in the summertime and everyone will complain about "la canicule" (the heat wave), these days are usually very limited in number.

| 29) | Don't expect to do much sunbathing in Paris. |

Even though you may see a sunny Paris in films and in pictures, it is total fiction. I even burst out laughing recently when I saw someone trying to promote sunbathing in Paris. I'd say "Bon courage" (good luck) trying to accomplish that.

Parisians dream of the beaches in sunny parts of the world, which is why they started a phenomenon called Paris Plage a few years ago, but that doesn't change the fact that sunshine is not always "au rendez-vous." During the summer, the city authorities bring in sand and create a beach-like atmosphere along the Seine, probably for the misfortunate souls who cannot go south on vacation where all the real sunshine is. They may try to create a vacation atmosphere but they can't control the weather.

It actually rains one day out of every three in Paris on the average. Never forget to take an umbrella with you, because you will need it. You will be using your umbrella much more than your suntan lotion.

French people love the sunshine, which is why most of them head southward whenever they get a chance, because that's where they can do some serious sunbathing. In the summer, when everyone is on vacation, they flock to the Riviera and all of southern France or head to Spain where they can bask in the sunshine to their hearts' content.

When I decided to sell my apartment in the Parisian suburbs years ago, I was contacted by a potential buyer who came at least five times to try to check out where there was sunshine in my apartment. After the first couple of times, he was starting to become desperate. He was convinced that there must certainly be a ray of sunlight somewhere, and I said to myself that he must not have been from around Paris, because he would know better. My son ended up calling him "Monsieur Soleil" (Mr. Sunshine) because every time he came, he looked for those rays of light and there was, of course, no sunshine. What did he expect? It was Paris.

30)	Develop new habits in the bathroom.

Most bathrooms do not have a shower curtain or even any type of structure to hang up a curtain. Usually you have a hand-held showerhead with a hose and you can either sit in the tub to take a shower or use the bathtub to take a bath. If you stand for your shower, you will probably need a mop for the water you splash on the floor.

The toilet will not be in the same room as the bathtub and sink and the bidet. That odd low sink next to the regular sink is a bidet and no, it is not for your feet. You can use it for your more private parts if you want. The toilet is always in a separate little room, and no, there is no sink in that room to wash your hands, so get over it and simply go to the bathroom to wash your hands afterwards.

If you want to buy a wash cloth in a regular store, you will only find "un gant de toilette" – a type of glove that you use as a wash cloth.

| 31) | Say hello and goodbye appropriately. |

Until the days of the 2020 pandemic and lockdown and quarantine ("le confinement" in French), French people would always shake hands to say hello to greet you, and also to say goodbye to you when leaving. Closer friends would kiss each other on the cheeks – "faire les bises" - and depending on what region of France you were from, you would exchange either two, three or four kisses on the cheeks. Girls will kiss each other on the cheeks, a girl and boy will do the same, but two boys together usually shake hands. The pandemic has changed these habits, and hand gestures are used more often these days, but who knows, maybe after the pandemic, French people will go back to shaking hands and giving out bises.

Most Americans are not used to shaking hands all the time and especially getting kissed all the time. Years ago, I arranged for a young American college student to stay with a neighbor who was around the same age as the American girl. My neighbor, who wanted to welcome the American girl with open arms and of course give her some "bises" on her cheeks, approached the girl when she walked through the door. The poor American girl didn't know what to think of this French girl who was getting closer and closer to her, with her lips puckered, and she

started backing up and looked like she was trying to find
the door to make her escape until I explained to her this
French tradition.

32)	Forget your bacon and eggs for breakfast.

Don't expect cereal, bacon and eggs, French toast (no,
French toast is not French), pancakes, toast, orange juice
and coffee for breakfast. Forget the donuts and bagels too.
You won't find maple syrup either. You will still have your
coffee but if you are at home, it will be served in a bowl –
yes, the French like to have a big amount of coffee in the
morning and it makes it easier to dip your croissant or
baguette into it.

Instead of your American-style breakfast, you will come
to appreciate continental breakfasts with strong, fresh
French coffee (served in a bowl, of course, at home) with
cream and sugar if you so desire, and either "une tartine"
– French bread and butter that usually is covered with
some type of delicious jam – or a croissant (or even two)
or an apple turnover called "un chausson aux pommes"
or a buttery roll with a stick of chocolate in the middle
called "un pain au chocolat." You will immediately forget
your bacon and eggs when you smell the delicious
fragrance of these fresh-baked goods that can be found
everywhere and every day in your local boulangerie that
is just around the corner.

One unusual item I discovered for breakfast in France
is called "biscotte." The first time I saw it years ago, I
didn't quite know what to think of it. It looks like a small
piece of dried up bread that is crunchy like a cracker, but
it is thicker and bigger than a cracker. I had a roommate
years ago when I was a student who would get out the
box every day, make herself a bowl of coffee over a gas
Bunser burner that she used in our dorm room, and
spread butter and orange marmalade over this biscotte.
Somehow she managed to smoothly spread the butter

and jam over the surface, unlike me, who could never do so without breaking the biscotte into pieces. I developed a taste for these things after a while and I finally became skilled at putting my butter and jam on them as well. You can find them in any grocery store or supermarket, so get some and give it a try.

33)	Don't try to figure out French humor or use the needle.

The French draw humor from criticism. They like to criticize by poking fun at someone or something, and their sense of humor is sometimes called the French needle. French humor, however, is a tricky subject. What you find funny, they might not find funny at all. What they find funny may leave you wondering why they are all laughing. For example, in movies, they like to see people leaning forward making some muscular arm gestures in front of them and walking and rolling their butts. They find that hilarious. I am still wondering what is so funny about a rolling butt.

Some of France's more satirical newspapers such as "Charlie Hebdo" and "Le canard enchaîné" have always used mockery and sarcasm in their articles, which, in recent years, has strained their relations with some other countries and groups of people who found their articles offensive instead of humorous. These two particular newspapers have been around for decades and are known for their sharp, biting wit.

Humor, of course, changes and evolves with time. Back in the day, in the U.S., we had comedians like Jerry Lewis and in France, they had a very popular actor named Louis de Funès. Since these times, France has produced many very funny movies that you can probably find online these days. One of my favorites is "Astérix et Obélix: Mission Cléopatre" which is full of play-on-words that you will eventually come to appreciate once you have mastered the language. Another old favorite is "La chèvre" with Pierre Richard and Gérard Depardieu, which is a funny story about the most unlucky man on the face of the earth.

More recently, "Bienvenue chez les Ch'tis" has become another favorite. This is an amusing and heartwarming story about a French postal employee who is transferred to the North of France where it is cold and there is no sunshine instead of being sent to the South filled with sunshine, where he dreamed of being, just like most French people.

If you want to better understand what the French needle is, look at the comedy called "Le dîner des cons." It's a story about a man who invites stupid people with stupid hobbies to dinners with his friends so they can all make fun of the guest behind his back.

There is also lighter humor. Petit Nicolas stories are very popular in France and movies such as "Le Petit Nicolas" and "Les vacances du Petit Nicolas" will make you smile.

34)	Don't expect to understand French movie endings.

In the U.S., a lot of people like to see movies that are either filled with action or romance or an adventure of some kind and most American movies these days are filled with all kinds of special effects. You have a beginning situation, a development of this situation and then the ending to the situation. Most Americans I know like to have clear-cut endings that bring all the events to some kind of conclusion. Usually we like happy endings with everything neatly arranged or some kind of triumph over some problem or obstacle.

Do not expect French movies to follow this trend. In some cases, depending, of course, on the type of movie, you will see a reflection of French life, often with people sitting at a table and eating, because this is a huge part of French culture. You may have some sort of romantic involvement and maybe a couple of bedroom scenes, and there will be some type of development of the story. But you will not be given an ending to the story. Many times it will be up to you to imagine what happens afterwards, which many Americans find is not an ending at all since it is not given to you directly and we are not used to having to dream up our own endings. It's not true of all French movies, but it is the case in many instances and whenever I showed one of these movies in my French classes at school, my students would always look at me afterwards and say, "That's it?" with astonishment.

There are many wonderful, interesting French films and some that will leave you wondering about what happens next. You have classics that have been around for decades and are still popular in France and many others that are more recent. There are quite a few that are based on true events or use history as the backdrop to the story.

Some very popular films that I showed in schools include the following: "Cyrano de Bergerac" (a wonderful classic by Edmond Rostand and a beautiful film with a tragic love story in the 17th century), "Indochine" (a love story that takes place during the war in Indochina), "Intouchables" (a heartwarming story about a down-and-out personal aide hired to help a handicapped Frenchman, based on true events), "La vie en rose" (based on the true story of the French singer Edith Piaf), "Coco avant Chanel" (the life story of fashion designer Coco Chanel), "Au revoir, les enfants" (based on a true story about France under German Occupation during World War II), "Le père Goriot" (one of Balzac's classic novels criticizing Parisian high society in the 19th century), "Madame Bovary" (based on Flaubert's 19th century novel), among many others. "Jean de Florette" and its sequel "Manon des sources" are two films worth your time, but watch out for a couple of scenes that are not for the faint-hearted.

35)	Learn to drink wine or mineral water.

Most people prefer wine with their meals. French people definitely prefer wine and there are so many different ones to choose from that it's no problem to find one you really like. You can buy wine and alcohol at your local supermarket and nobody is going to be checking your ID to know your age when you make the purchase. If you are not a wine drinker, you can choose to have mineral water instead, and there is a wide variety of mineral water everywhere, both bubbly and plain, like Badoit or Perrier or Evian, just to name a few. If you go to a fast food restaurant, you will not find wine, but if you go to a traditional French restaurant, you will not be having soda or tea or coffee or milk or any type of soft drink with your meal. You could, of course, order these drinks, but you will be shocking some of your waiters who are used to serving wine or water with the meal.

There appears to be no specific time to start drinking wine during the daytime. Year ago, when I taught English and beginning Russian at a French telephone company, I would go to a café across the street from where I was teaching, and I would always be surprised to find some French technicians from the company having their "petit rouge" – a small glass of red wine – before going to work. What a way to start the work day. No, I stuck to coffee, thank you. Maybe it didn't affect a lot of my colleagues out of habit, but I tend to doze off after a glass of wine and wanted to be awake for what I had to do during the day.

36)	Don't smile too much, especially in public.

People will think you are weird if you smile too much.

They will look around, and wonder what is so funny. Americans, especially American women like myself, love to smile, but you will be out of place amidst all the stone-faced passengers on the metro or bus or the train. Parisians who come to the U.S. have the opposite problem because they do not smile spontaneously like most Americans do, and sometimes Americans think the Parisians are not friendly. In reality, they are friendly but they are not going to flash you any smiles, at least not right away.

37)	Don't go to the wrong floor.

Someone may tell you to go to what you think is the third floor - le troisième - and you go up to the third floor and knock on the door and a total stranger opens it up, because you got the floors wrong. The French start with the ground floor, le rez-de-chaussée, and then start counting, which means the American first floor is the French ground floor, the American second floor is the French first floor, and so on. If you are a student and they happen to tell you that you will be living in a tiny room "au sixième étage sans ascenseur," be prepared to walk up six flights of steps to the seventh floor.

38)	Get used to living without an elevator.

If you are a student living in one of these tiny rooms perched at the top of an old apartment building, you should realize that you will have to walk up flights of steps and also carry your books, your groceries, your furniture, your suitcases, your sports equipment and whatever else you use up and down these old stairways. You will be living in "une chambre de bonne" – a maid's room - what used to be servants' quarters when well-to-do families had domestic helpers in their homes. Most of these rooms are tiny, maybe about 10 feet by 10 feet, and only have a sink for you to wash up, so comfort is very limited. Most of these rooms have low rent, but there is a reason for the low rent.

If you are living in an old apartment building or even one that is fairly recent, there may not be an elevator either. Some of the old apartment buildings have ancient, rickety wrought-iron lifts that are not big enough to fit more than two or three people and forget about any large suitcases or furniture you may have. The suitcases and furniture will have to be hauled up the staircases which can either be in marble and sweeping and majestic or narrow and worn, depending on the age and construction of the building.

Years ago, I had quite a time with French elevators. For lunch, I once met an American woman who was a former boss of mine when she came to Paris, and we had lunch at an elegant restaurant in a beautiful hotel called Hôtel Royal Monceau, just down the street from the Champs-Elysées. Just before the lunch, a motorcycle happened to whiz by her on the street, making her fall and break her ankle (yes, by the way, watch out for whizzing motorcyles in the street). Her foot was so swollen by the time we finished lunch that I had to call the hotel concierge to have a wheelchair take her to her room. The regular elevator was, of course, so small that we had to use the cargo elevator to get to the room. I ended up having to wheel her down the street to a medical center, and of course, the wheelchair would not fit into the medical center elevator. She ended up hopping around on one foot to get into the elevator, go upstairs for an X-ray and then hop back down the hallway to the elevator. After that, I had to take her to a doctor's office on the other side of the city. The wheelchair somehow folded up to fit into the trunk of the cab we took, but the wood and wrought-iron entrance gate to the building and the wrought-iron elevator at the doctor's office were more obstacles. Once again, she had to hop around without the wheelchair.

This could be you, so be prepared.

39)	Don't expect to live in a large home.

Homes in Paris are much smaller than what you will usually find in the U.S. There are very few houses inside Paris, so you will be looking at apartments that are generally old and always pricey by American standards. If you plan to live in the suburbs, you can find houses, and many American companies will help you find a home, usually to the west of Paris, since they are the ones paying for it if you happen to be transferred to Paris for a while. Regardless of whether you choose an apartment or a house, homes are always much smaller than what you find in the U.S. In the older apartment buildings, you may not have enough room to sit in the kitchen and have breakfast, because kitchens in these types of buildings are very small. If you are in a building that was built within the last fifty years, you may have better chances of having a larger kitchen, but the overall area of the home will still be less than what you are used to. Some older houses have very low ceilings, so if you are over 5 foot 7, you may have to bend down a little to go into the house.

40)	Don't expect restaurant portions to be large.

Just like for houses, food portions in restaurants are much smaller than in the U.S., generally because the cost of living is high in Paris and food is very expensive. You are not going to get those thick steaks that you see in American steakhouses or the large servings of side dishes you are probably used to. You will be exchanging quantity for quality because French cuisine offers a wide variety of marvelous dishes that are carefully prepared. You will be savoring the wonderful taste, but you just won't be eating as much as in the U.S.

In some cases, you may even hesitate to eat the tiny portion you see on your plate, because presentation is key in French cuisine and the food almost looks like artwork.

41)	No snacking in between meals.

When French people come to the U.S., they always have the impression that Americans are eating all the time. We always have cookies or popcorn or chips or a candy bar lying around, and most of us like to nibble once in a while, regardless of what time it is. Most French people will have their continental breakfast, lunch, coffee and a pastry of some kind around 4 p.m. for "le goûter" and then dinner. I was always surprised to see that if my French friends wanted to snack on something, they would grab a piece of fruit – an apple or a pear or a tangerine. Otherwise, their eating is pretty much limited to what they have at mealtimes, which is probably part of their secret to keeping their weight down.

42)	Eat dinner between 7 p.m. and 10 p.m.

There are no early bird specials in Paris and some restaurants close between 2 p.m. and 7 p.m. Many restaurants close at 10 p.m. during normal times. The pandemic and curfews raised havoc for many bars, cafés and restaurants, but hopefully we will get back to what life was before the pandemic. Cafés are usually open much longer, but you can generally only get small dishes or sandwiches there, not the full course meals you find in traditional French restaurants. French people have dinner much later than Americans, usually between 7 p.m. and 10 p.m. They sometimes like to have long lunch times, usually between noon and 2 p.m. Most of them will have "le goûter" around 4 p.m. to help them hold out until the later dinner times.

43)	Keep a lot of money for gasoline for your car.

Keep a lot of money for gasoline if you have a car, because you are going to need it. Gas is usually at least twice the price it is in the U.S. and sometimes much more. It's no wonder that French cars are so small. There are a lot of other means of transportation that are cheaper. You can even rent a bike if you want, or if you own a motorcycle, it is a way to easily get around the city, even though you have to be very careful of traffic. Buses run throughout the city and the métro and RER provide excellent means to get around.

It is actually very easy to find your way around by métro. Maps of all the lines are posted everywhere in the subway entrances and you can find your way around by looking at the last station of each line to know the name of the line. You find your location on the map, the station where you are standing, and you look at which direction you need to go on the line from where you are. When you walk down the hallway, you will see entrances to platforms bearing the name of the direction it is going. Voilà. C'est simple! There's nothing to it, and it is easier and less expensive than using a car.

If you are staying in Paris for an extended length of time, you should consider getting a pass that allows you to use all the public transportation within the city limits for a lump-sum price for the month. You can get around the city for one single price for the month and do not have to buy tickets every time you go somewhere using public transportation.

44)	Avoid toilets in some of the older cafés.

Don't be surprised by some of the toilets you find in older cafés. You may go into the stall and wonder where the toilet went. Then you look at the floor and see there is a spot for your two feet and a hole in between. That, my friend, is what they call a Turkish toilet. I don't think they even exist in the U.S., and if they did, they probably would have been banned.

45)	Always lock your door when you go out.

Paris is Paris and a big city with all kinds of people, including people who may want to take what you have in your home or in your pockets. Some Parisians install special reinforced steel doors to their homes to be sure than nobody can break in. If you are offered an apartment on the ground floor or even one floor up, I would suggest that you have second thoughts about taking it. I knew someone who had an apartment on the second floor of an apartment building in a quiet part of the city. He went to work in the morning, but when he returned home at the end of the day, someone had broken in and removed almost every single item he owned. They took his bed, his clothes, his chairs and table, his sofa, his dishes, his television and stereo, his food and wine. It was as if someone had come with a moving van and hauled everything away. The thieves took everything except his toothbrush. I guess they didn't want a used toothbrush.

I myself got robbed of money only one time during the 23 years I lived in Paris. I was on an escalator at La Défense, watching my son who was small at the time and not giving my full attention to my purse which was dangling by my side. It was when I went to pull my wallet out of my purse a short while later and didn't find it that I realized that the person who had pushed his way around me on the escalator had been pushing around me for a reason. After that, I used cross body bags and kept the purse in front of me.

When you go to a café or a restaurant, watch your belongings as well. I had an umbrella once that I put down next to my chair and when I went to pick it up when leaving, it had vanished into thin air.

You have to also be careful getting on and off subways. Years ago, little kids would push their way around people to get on and off the métro just to distract them, and sometimes these people would be minus their wallets by the time they got off.

I used to work in an office with a friend who loved to buy very expensive clothing and shoes. We worked down the street from shops in the high-fashion area of the city. She was always in style and found a pair of beautiful boots that she paid $800 for. This was many, many years ago, so that was a lot of money, especially at that time. I must say that the boots were absolutely magnificent, but they must have drawn unwanted attention, because my poor friend came into the office one day and was miserable. I found out that someone had broken into her apartment and all they took were her $800 boots.

46)	Drop American football for other sports.

Soccer, "le football," is the most popular sport in France. American football is called "le football américain" to distinguish it from soccer. You are not going to find football games or baseball games in Paris. You may occasionally find some basketball, but it is rare. Sports in martial arts, like judo and taekwando, are popular. A lot of French people like swimming too. Rugby is also very popular and rugby games are often broadcast on television. Fencing is prevalent too, but soccer and soccer games remain the major attraction in sports. You also have le Tour de France bicycle race every year since cycling is very popular. If you are a tennis fan, you are in luck because every year there is the French Open tournament at Roland-Garros in Paris.

Horse racing is also popular and there is a race track at Vincennes and another one at Auteuil. Every Sunday many Parisians buy tickets for le Tiercé.

If you are a parent and think your child is going to get

a scholarship for sports at school in France, think again. Schools in France are reserved for studies and there are no sports teams at schools. The same applies to music. For sports, you will need to go to a private club or get accepted into a professional training organization, and for music, you will need to enroll in a music conservatory.

You are not going to see cheerleaders in France. The French refer to them as "les pom pom girls" because they don't have any but know what they are.

47)	Remember that not all parts of Paris are suitable for kids.

Like practically all cities, there are sections of Paris you should avoid, especially if you are taking students or young children with you. I would suggest that you avoid the woods to the west of Paris at night. Le Bois de Boulogne has a reputation of being a hotspot when the sun goes down and not the safest place to be. You are fine most of the time during the day, but not after nightfall.

Certain streets near the cabaret Moulin Rouge in Montmartre and Pigalle should also be avoided at night, if you are alone or with children. I found out that one of my teaching colleagues who accompanied students to Paris one year unknowingly took students to this area towards nightfall. It was not the type of education she was looking to provide them with.

With time, you will learn which districts – "arrondissements" – of Paris are safe in general. The city is divided into 20 arrondissements, each of which has its own "mairie" or town hall for the district. The 5th arrondissement is where you will find the Sorbonne and a lot of college students and shops and small restaurants and cafés of all kinds. The 6th arrondissement has the famous café "Les Deux Magots" and shops and churches and a lot of apartments in old buildings, and tends to be one of the safer parts of the city. The 8th arrondissement includes the Arch of Triumph and the Champs-Elysées, which generally are safe areas of the city. The 17th and 15th and 14th arrondissements are more residential and are normally areas that are safe. The 7th arrondissement contains the Eiffel Tower, Napoleon's tomb and a military museum and is mostly residential, so they tend to be calm. The 16th arrondissement has the reputation of being one of the most chic places to live in Paris, and undoubtedly the most expensive as well.

If you want to go to Chinatown, you need to go to the 13th arrondissement. Many Asians from France's former colony of Indochina came to Paris and basically stayed together in this arrondissement. You will find all types of Chinese restaurants and grocery stores selling oriental food supplies.

48)	Know what you are eating.

French cuisine is absolutely wonderful, but there are certain foods you may not want to try. I have had snails smothered in butter and garlic and parsley sauce, and savored every one of them, but some people may not be so enthusiastic about trying snails. You will be given the prepared snail in a shell and will be given a small fork to pull it out and eat it. When prepared the way they should be, they are delicious and you should try them.

Frog's legs may also be on the menu, but I must admit that it is something that never tempted me, but it may be different for you.

Horse meat is another food that I have never wanted to try, but you can buy some at specialized shops called "Chevalines" and in some supermarkets.

Ask what you are being served before you eat it. Sometimes you may not want to know, but you can always refuse politely, at least with French people. Some dishes that you may not want to try include tripes – the intestines of an animal or organs such as the tongue or liver or brain. Years ago, I was going to try tongue at the resto u (university cafeteria) but it looked too much like a big fat tongue staring up at me from the plate. Never again.

If you are offered "steak tartare" and decide to have it, know that you are not having a steak. I hope you like raw hamburger with a raw egg on the top because that's what "steak tartare" is.

| 49) | Buy your groceries in different stores. |

Many French people look for quality food products when it comes to preparing their meals at home, and they will go to the market or to different specialty shops. You can buy your fruit and vegetables at the fruit and vegetable store and some wine or mineral water at your local épicerie. You can buy your meat at the boucherie. You buy your bread at the boulangerie. You can buy fish at the poissonnerie. You can buy cheese and dairy products at the crémerie. You can buy ham or pork products at the charcuterie or what I call the "pork shop" because all you can buy there is pork products and maybe just a small mixed salad. You'll find your pastry for the goûter or dessert at the pâtisserie. If you want flowers to decorate your house or to put on your dinner table or to offer as a gift, you will go chez le fleuriste – to the flower shop.

| 50) | Take a grocery bag with you. |

If you go to the supermarket, they will give you a plastic bag like you get in the U.S., even though most Parisians and French people will take a bag with them called "un filet" that is a type of rope bag or a grocery cart with a handle, canvas bag and wheels called "un cabas." If you go to a smaller grocery store, like the local corner store –

"l'épicerie" -, you will not be given a bag. You are expected to bring your own. The same applies when you go to your local open-air market that usually takes place two or three times a week. If you forget your bag, you are going to have a hard time taking all your groceries home.

51)	Pay less for groceries at supermarkets

If you are concerned about your budget for food or if you are pressed for time and do not want to go to a number of specialty shops for whatever you need, you can go to supermarkets. Stores like Auchan, Monoprix, Franprix, Leclerc and Carrefour are chain supermarkets where you can buy all your groceries and much more at the same time. Some of them are the equivalent of Walmart in the U.S. and they sell not only groceries but also clothing, cosmetics, books and many other items. Monoprix has been around for decades, since 1932 when it was founded. Auchan was started a number of years later, in 1951. Leclerc started up in 1948 and Franprix has existed since 1957.

Casino is not a casino, so don't expect to go inside and find slot machines and game tables. It is the name of another very popular chain supermarket. Casino's origins go back about a century and it has grown into a gigantic multi-national company since then.

52)	Don't expect to be carded when you order a drink.

Even though it appears there are some regulations in France about drinking age which is officially 18 or 16 if a parent agrees on it, nobody is going to ask to see your ID to find out your age when you order an alcoholic drink. You can buy wine and alcohol in grocery stores without showing ID as well. If you are a high school student on a school trip with your American school, however, the American rules are going to apply to you since you are with your group and you would need special permission from your parents to do some wine-tasting or alcohol-drinking during your trip.

Don't expect to find stores devoted only to liquor in France either. Some states in the U.S. still have liquor stores and strict regulations about who can purchase alcoholic, but in France and in grocery stores you find everywhere in Paris, you can buy wine and alcohol.

53)	Think "Nude is natural."

Almost every French movie you see seems to have nude people walking around in it, even films that are comedies and intended for children, which was always a problem at the school where I taught in the U.S. I'd have to fast forward through parts or try to block the view of the screen by standing in front of it or not show a certain film at all for this reason.

Nudity, however, is just about everywhere in Paris. All you have to do is go to the museums or look at some of the many statues in the street.

If you go to a cabaret like "Moulin Rouge" or the "Lido" or if you even watch a TV program I loved to watch called "Le plus grand cabaret du monde" with Patrick Sébastien doing the presenting, you will see lots of feathers and lots of topless ladies. French TV companies used to broadcast shows from the Crazy Horse Saloon for New Years' celebrations every year and you would see very artistic shows starring ladies with not many clothes on.

If you happen to go to a public pool in Paris or in the neighboring suburbs and if it is one of those rare days when the sun happens to be shining in the summer, you will see topless lady sunbathers lying around.

54)	Learn to talk like a French person using understatements.

You will find that many French people like to use understatements to express a point of view. For example, instead of saying someone is ugly, you say they are not beautiful. If someone is fat, you say the person is not very thin. If they are very short, you are going to say they are not tall at all. If they are stupid, you say they ain't smart.

55)	Talk with your hands.

French people use many more hand gestures than Americans do. They are not as articulate in hand language as Italians are, but they are pretty close. French people from the South of France probably use more gestures than Parisians generally do, but hands and arms still fly around in the City of Light. Swipe your hand over your head and say "J'en ai marre" or "J'en ai ras le bol" to show your frustration and declare, "I'm fed up." Show a thumbs up and say "C'est bien" (that's good). Extend your hand and flip it over a couple of times when asked how you are and reply with "Comme ci, comme ça" (Just so-so). These are just a few. You will be able to learn all of them from simple observation.

The meaning of most hand gestures is obvious, especially if you happen to come across a Parisian suffering from road rage. You may witness a couple of Frenchmen jumping out of their cars and gesticulating and yelling at each other, but all of a sudden, they will calm down and get back into their cars as if nothing had happened. There will be a lot of noise and hand movements but nothing more.

56)	Take cash with you to public places.

If you are in a park or a museum or another public
place in Paris and you need to use the bathroom, you may
see a lady waiting near the door with a small dish on
which you are supposed to leave a tip. Generally this
happens only in public places, but there are more and
more facilities called "sanisettes," some of which you still
have to pay for and some of which are free. If you are a
customer in a café, you can use their restroom, but even
then, there are certain places where they expect you to
leave a little cash.

In some parks, like the Jardin du Luxembourg,
somebody will come around to ask you to pay for the park
chair you are sitting on. The wood benches are free, but
not the chairs.

57)	Avoid embarrassing mistakes in French

Do not say "Je suis pleine" (for a girl) or "je suis plein"
(for a guy) if you want to say you're full. You are saying
you are pregnant in this case. The right expression is Je
n'ai plus faim (I'm no longer hungry).

You do not say "I'm done" by saying "Je suis fini." That
means you are dead. The right expression is "J'ai fini."

When you want to go to the restroom, you are not going
to ask for the "salle de bains" – the "bathroom." The "salle
de bains" for a French person is where you take a shower
or have baths – it is literally the "bath room.". In English,
most of us want to be a little refined and not talk about
the "toilet" but the word does not have the same
connotation for a French person. On top of that, there is
not just one toilet when you go to the restroom, but
several, so the French ask where "the toilets" are. "Où
sont les toilettes?" is what you need to ask when you ask
about a restroom.

I suggest that you avoid swear words as well, and

believe me, you will pick up this vocabulary very quickly. Swearing in a foreign language does not feel like swearing until you are given the translation of what you said and realize what words have come out of your mouth... What? Did I really say that?

58)	Never say there is a more beautiful city than Paris.

Parisians will tear you apart and they are right to do so. Look around you. Everything is symmetrical, even trees are sometimes cut to be completely in line with each other. Art is everywhere and the statues are numerous and beautiful. There is beauty everywhere, and maybe some ugliness in some spots, but let's just ignore that. Where else can you see a magnificent cathedral called Notre Dame that builders took 200 years to construct. Walk down « la plus belle avenue du monde » - les Champs-Elysées – with its wide sidewalks, elegant shops and wonderful cafés. Even if you don't have a dime in your pocket, you can walk down the most beautiful street in the world and appreciate the beauty around you. All the monuments, like the Arch of Triumph and Concorde Square with its sculpted fountains are worth the walk. L'Opéra and the surrounding neighborhood are wonderful to see as well. Go to Montmartre which is on a hill and see a fantastic view of the city. Take a stroll along boulevard Saint-Michel in the Latin Quarter and go to the Luxembourg Gardens or walk along the Seine River. The sights of beauty are endless and what's even better is that they are free.

When the Montparnasse tower – that big 59-story skyscraper that sticks out from everything else in the 15th arrondissement – was built many years ago, Parisians decided they did not want any more of those things in their city. You will find some towers that have 20 or 25 stories in the 13th arrondissement, towards the outskirts of the city, but aside from these few apartment buildings, there are no skyscrapers within the city limits. To most Parisians, la Tour Montparnasse is an eye-sore and they will not put up with any more of them, which is why you will not see buildings that are more than 7 stories high. The fact that almost all the buildings in Paris are the same height also adds to the beauty of the place and gives you the impression that you are more in a town than a city.

You will, however, find towers and skyscrapers just outside the city to the west at La Défense, which is a large commercial center. This is a business and commercial area that was built in more recent years, starting in the 1970's, and contains mostly offices, a mall, restaurants, a movie theater and an exhibition hall. La Grande Arche – that huge arch that looks like a gigantic cube – was built in recent ti;es and contains offices. Parisians, however, did not lose their sense of beauty when building the Grande Arche: if you look through the Arch of Triumph in Paris facing west and with your back towards the Champs-Elysées, you will see the Grande Arche in the distance and realize that both arches are perfectly aligned.

59)	Don't be surprised to see machine guns on the street.

Paris is a city with all types of people who will go on strike, protest, demonstrate and show the whole world that they are very unhappy about something. I suggest that you avoid any streets that have demonstrators because their protests sometimes get out of hand and the military police, equipped with machine guns and billy clubs, steps in. If you do get involved somehow in these protests and they catch you doing something you should not be doing, you might be put on the first plane out of Paris and be told not come back if you are not a French national.

In addition to this, there have always been terrorists in Paris, even though in more recent years, people seem to have become much more aware of them, because, unlike many years ago, when they used to target only certain political figures or specific groups, they now hit people and places blindly. The regular police handle everyday security, but they can call in the national military police called the CRS (Compagnies républicaines de sécurité) who are the ones with the machine guns for major demonstrations that could get out of control or for incidents that involve violence. The CRS will show up in vans and will be wearing combat uniforms with bullet-proof vests and full-body protective padding and helmets with a face guard, and they will be carrying a shield, a club and guns.

Years ago, when I was a student, there were always confrontations between political party members who were students at the political science branch of the University of Paris located on rue d'Assas. They were all so politically-minded that right-wing students would sit on the right-hand side of the classroom and left-wing students would sit on the left. Since there were so many clashes between the groups, the CRS would just camp out in their vans on a nearby street next to Luxembourg Garden. They were always there, ready to intervene.

The CRS is always around, but there are times when they cannot foresee everything. One day, for example, years later, I was walking down the street with my ex-husband and we thought about getting a newspaper, but we decided not to and continued on down the street. Not even five minutes later, we heard a huge explosion and shattered glass falling. Back in the day, there was a German terrorist group that was active in Paris, and they had placed a bomb near a building we had walked by. One person lost his life and several other pedestrians were injured from flying glass. I will always remember that day and am thankful that we had decided we didn't want to read a newspaper.

German terrorists at that time also happened to put a bomb in Goethe Institute where I was taking German lessons. The bomb was found in the ladies' bathroom, and after that, the CRS was there for security checks whenever you went into the building. That put an end to my German lessons. I wanted to learn German but not that badly.

A few years later, when I was working with a company in the 8th arrondissement, I was in a building with other companies and organizations on other floors. One of these organizations was the Palestinian Liberation Organization. When I came back from my one-month vacation one year, I returned to this office to find it surrounded by the CRS with their machine guns, because there had been a shooting in the building. Welcome back to Paris.

In that same office on another occasion, I happened to answer a creepy phone call saying that there was a bomb in the building. The monotone voice on the phone gave the name of the previous company that had moved out of our offices, and I tried to tell them that it was a mistake, but then I realized it was a recording and not a person on the line. Somebody from the office reported the incident to the police, and the building had to be evacuated, and bomb-sniffing dogs were brought in, but no bomb was found. I still remember how the president of the company, a "Pied Noir" – a Frenchman who had lived in North Africa and who had survived the French-Algerian War but had been deported from Algeria after his company had been seized – refused to be intimidated by a bomb threat and continued working all the time the CRS was searching the building. The threat was just a threat, but it was taken seriously.

Many years later, when I was accompanying a group of high school students on a trip to France, we were all in line at Roissy Airport, ready to check our bags in for our return trip to the U.S., when everyone in the airport was told to evacuate the building. The CRS, with machine guns and full attire, appeared, because a piece of luggage had been abandoned at the airport, and whenever that is the case and there is any suspicion of a bomb, the CRS will be called in. They removed the bag and exploded it themselves out on the street. It was no bomb but somebody probably lost his set of traveling clothes. By the way, never leave your suitcase unattended at the airport.

60)	Don't say "Thank you" to a compliment.

You can thank a French person for anything they give to you or for something he or she may do for you, but they will find it weird if they make some compliment to you and you say thanks. Instead, you are supposed to express some type of astonishment by saying, for example, "Oh, do you really think so?" ("Vous trouvez?") or "Ah, vraiment?" (Oh really?). If you say "Thank you," they won't understand what you are thanking them for.

On the same note, don't expect French people to compliment you all the time. They don't hand out compliments easily, but when they do, it is very sincere.

61)	See French movies in a theater but forget the nachos.

Once you have learned some basic French, go and see a movie in a movie theater. There are many "cinémas" in Paris, and you can now find lists online. At your local newsstand, you can still find "L'Officiel des spectacles" and "Pariscope" which are two weekly publications that tell you everything that is going on in Paris and where to go for restaurants, movies, plays, concerts, museums and exhibits, cabarets and children's activities and any special events happening in Paris.

In the movie theaters, ushers used to show you to your

seat, but in some more modern facilities, the ushers may
not be around and you can sit wherever you wish. You
will not see spectators eating all the junk food you see in
American movie theaters either. The French generally
don't eat outside of meals, and you do not have the large
concession stands you see in movie theaters in the U.S.
Years ago, there weren't even any concession stands: one
of the ushers would walk around with a tray that had a
strap around her neck, and she would sell candy bars or
small ice cream bars on a stick. I also found that French
people tended to be considerate of others and were raised
that way: they are not going to disturb you with any noise
or food odors while you are in the same room with them
to watch a movie and they expect you to do the same.

62)	Learn to deal with people of many different origins.

According to 2021 statistics, about 35% of the people
living in Paris are immigrants or the children of
immigrants. Most of them are from former French
colonies and lived in countries where the French built
their schools and taught them French or are descendants
of immigrants from these countries. Many are from North
Africa, from the Maghreb – Algeria, Morocco and Tunisia.
Others may be from former colonies like Senegal, Mali,
the Ivory Coast, just to name a few.

Many Asians also live in Paris and moved to this city
after the disintegration of the old French Indochina that
was comprised of Cambodia, Laos and Vietnam. A very
large number immigrated to France after the fall of
Vietnam and Cambodia to Communist rule after 1975.

People of other nationalities have also settled in Paris
and brought with them their traditions, beliefs and
culture. There is a Russian community in the 17th
arrondissement consisting of descendants of Russians
who fled the Russian Revolution over 100 years ago. A

Russian Orthodox Church is still attended in that community.

People of all types of nationalities have come to Paris as evidenced by the number of foreign restaurants and specialty shops in the city. Many have kept the traditions of the countries they come from and in many cases, adopted the customs of France as well. Just as in the U.S., they tend to live near each other in their communities.

What is wonderful about having such diverse communities in Paris is that you can buy food, supplies and other items that you would not find elsewhere in the many small shops and stores and stands they run.

63)	Don't be upset when people cut in front of you in line.

For some reason there are certain Parisians who like to cut in front of you when you are standing in line. I don't know why, but it happens very often. There are a number of French people who don't take rules seriously and they are always trying to bend them. Some will park cars where they are not supposed to and they don't care if they have to pay a fine – or maybe they just throw the fines away. Others will totally ignore speed limits, yet others will decide that they are not going to waste their time standing in a long line. Even income tax is sometimes not taken very seriously in France, because it is not considered a federal offense.

64)	Get into the habit of having fruit for dessert.

Many French people love to have fruit instead of ice cream or cake or pudding or other nice and fattening desserts that we love here in the U.S. I learned to peel my apples the French way by turning the apple and carving

63

along the edge of the apple until you drop what looks like a ribbon into your plate. I learned how to remove orange rinds from oranges the French way by making five or six slice marks around the whole orange with a knife and then peeling the sections away by hand. I learned how to slice pears the French way by removing the skin and then cutting little slices to eat. Even fruit has a special technique.

65)	Don't expect to see a waitress serving you in a café.

All the servers in cafés and traditional French restaurants are men. Usually they wear white shirts and black pants. The men are there to do the heavy work and women are there to collect the money at the cash register. You may, very rarely, see a woman bring you over your coffee if she is the owner of the café or restaurant and wants to get to know you, but I personally recall having this happen to me only once in all the years I was in Paris, and it was special treatment because she wanted to ask for a favor.

66)	Don't be surprised by dogs sitting next to you in a café

Cafés are very dog friendly and many Parisians love their furry companions. Cafés allow them into the café and even onto the chairs in the café. I remember going to a café and sitting next to a Yorkshire terrier that kept sniffing in my direction.

What you do need to watch out for, though, is the doggy do in the streets. There are no laws saying Parisians have to pick up their doggy do, and even if there were laws for this, Parisians would probably just ignore them.

| 67) | Get an adapter for your electric devices. |

If you decide to bring any of your electric devices from the U.S., such as an electric razor or a hairdryer or an electric lamp or appliance like a coffee maker, make sure you have the converter that will allow you to use them in Paris. Most of the time you will not even be able to plug these devices directly into the outlet in France, so you will need the adapter that you can plug into the outlet and you can plug your device into the adapter. If you do not want to deal with an adapter, you can always go to a local store and purchase these items.

| 68) | Ignore the sales person following you around in a shop. |

One of the habits some of my American friends found the hardest to deal with was the fact that you cannot go into a small Parisian shop and just look around without a sales person standing next to you, waiting to make a sale. In the U.S., you can go into a store and sometimes you are lucky if you can even find a sales person somewhere. In Paris, in the boutiques, they will stick by your side, giving you the impression that you have walked into their store and now must buy something. They will offer you assistance, find what kind of item you are looking for, bend over backwards to find the right items just for you and to sell it to you. They will stick by your side until you finally walk out of the shop.

| 69) | Always be nice to your concierge. |

In every apartment building, there is a guardian who lives in an apartment on the ground floor, usually right near the entrance. This is your concierge. It may be a man or a woman with or without their families, but they are always present, every day, every hour of the day. This is the person who takes care of receiving and distributing your mail and packages. This is the person who handles all the maintenance and upkeep of the building. This is the person who sees everyone coming to see you and who knows what is going on in the building. Even though many Parisians think concierges have a reputation for being too nosy, that is part of their job. They are there, all the time, for you, so be nice to them.

| 70) | Don't expect to buy snacks at the drug store. |

In the U.S., when you go to a drug store, you can practically buy everything under the sun, from magazines and paper and envelopes to food and snacks and gifts. When you go to a drug store in France, you are going to exactly what it is called: "la Pharmacie." You will be able to find a few specialized items such as special shampoos that are usually for some kind of treatment and some creams for skin conditions, but everything you find in the pharmacy in Paris is related to medical conditions or healthcare. You can take your prescription from a doctor you will have found in Paris and get your prescription filled.

All pharmacies in France have a neon green cross sign on the front of them to make it easy for you to find them. Most of the cost of doctor's appointments and medicine is covered by French Social Security if you are enrolled in their program. Most French people have additional supplemental insurance through what is called "une mutuelle" to cover anything that might not be fully covered by French Social Security, so when you go to the pharmacy, you have practically nothing to pay or else you do pay something and get it fully reimbursed. Dental expenses are also covered by French Social Security, unlike the system in the U.S.

| 71) | Enjoy getting operations. |

Medical operations are also covered by French Social Security for those who are enrolled in it, so you do not have to worry about how to pay for it. Just like in the U.S., your employer will deduct charges from your pay for Social Security, but the difference in France is that it covers your medical expenses regardless of your age. Keep in mind, however, that it is a socialized system which means that for some major operations, the waiting period could be up to six months.

Maternity is covered 100% which includes any operation you may require for your delivery. Under the French system, if you work, you can be paid during your maternity leave, which is six weeks prior to the delivery date and ten weeks after the baby has arrived.

I had a major operation in Paris many years ago and did not have to pay anything at all. I had an excellent French surgeon who was also my doctor and who was very cavalier. He explained that he did the surgery in such a way that I would not have a scar that would be visible when I wore a bikini – not that I wore bikinis, but a lot of French women do. After the operation, being the gentlemen and kindly doctor he was, he told me that it was a pleasure to operate on me, to which I replied I hoped it would not become a habit.

| 72) | Don't get sick in July or August in Paris. |

Everything comes to a stop when it comes to vacation time in Paris. Almost everyone takes off in July and August, including doctors and medical staff. In France, vacation time is sacred and every French person who works for a company is entitled to five weeks of vacation, most of which is taken in either July or August for the entire month. Just about the only people you will see in Paris in July and August are tourists. Many stores in

Paris close for one or the other of the two months, and
even medical staff will not be replaced for these times,
even though you will be referred to someone in case of a
medical emergency.

July 1 and August 1 are the days of exodus of Parisians
just as July 31 and August 31 are the days of return.
Many years ago the French government started a traffic
program called "Bison fûté" to direct French drivers to
roads with fewer traffic jams in an attempt to alleviate the
kilometers and kilometers of backed-up traffic on the first
and last days of July and August. Departure hours and
alternate routes were proposed to Parisians eager to make
their way towards the sunny South. Parisians have
always been out to get their maximum days of vacation
which is why everyone in the city always ended up on the
highways at the same time. Don't expect them to change
their habits and delay their departures for a day or two.
They are too eager to get to that sunshine.

| 73) | Learn to ski and take off for les sports d'hiver. |

July and August are summer vacation times for
Parisians and the rest of France as well, but that last
week of the five-week vacation is devoted to going to the
mountains and generally going skiing in February. You
will be able to take the train like everyone else and find
all kinds of resorts in the Alps, the Vosges, Massif
Central, the Jura Mountains, or the Pyrenees.

| 74) | Don't get frustrated over school breaks. |

If you are a working parent with a child in a French
school, be prepared for school breaks which are much
more frequent throughout the school year in France than
in the U.S. If you have someone to watch over your child
while you are at work, then you do not have any problem,

but if you do not, you will need to figure out arrangements. School in France starts in September but there is a two-week break for All Saints' Day in November, two weeks for Christmas and New.Year's, two weeks in February for sports d'hiver, and two weeks in March or April for Easter. School runs until the end of June and then you have "les grandes vacances" – the two months of vacation everybody takes.

Not only are vacation breaks more numerous in French schools, the daily schedules change all the time, and schools start at around 8 a.m. but run much later than American schools, until around 4 p.m., except on Wednesdays, which are days off for most schools, and Saturday mornings, when there is a half day of school. Forget your weekend plans during the school year. However, you will have enough vacation breaks to make up for it.

If you are a student, just sit back and smile.

| 75) | Send your kid to a nature class. |

French schools are very different from American schools. Most American schools provide an occasional field trip that is maybe a half-day or a day long at the most. Some French schools, on the other hand, send their teachers and the whole class of students to places outside Paris for one, two or three weeks. They stay together all this time, they have classes together and they learn special skills, depending on the type of program it is. It could be "une classe de mer" and everyone would go to a place near the ocean to learn more about the sea. It could be "une classe poney" and everyone stays near a riding stable and learns how to ride and care for a pony or a horse. It could be "une classe de ski" for which everyone is sent to the mountains and learns how to ski. My son, who grew up in France, had the good fortune of being able to participate in all three of these programs when he was in elementary school. Not all classes are offered this opportunity and he was very lucky each time, but if it happens to be the case for you or your child, I suggest that you jump at the chance. Not only do students follow their regular school classes, but they learn to be more independent and can learn a lot through hands-on activities. The town hall will subsidize just about all the cost of the program to allow all the students to be able to participate, and all you or your child would need would be some extra pocket money and appropriate clothes purchased ahead of time.

76)	Be prepared to be oriented towards a specific profession.

By the time students in French schools reach high school, they have to make some very important choices about what type of job they want to have afterwards, because they will be enrolled in a specific study program for a specific "baccalauréat" – the notorious exam that students take at the end of their high school years and which allows them entry into colleges that specialize in the field they have chosen. Colleges that are subsidized by the government are practically free for students who have passed the "Bac" and the only cost involved are registration fees and eventually the cost of housing if a student is not near his home. The "Bac," however, is very stressful for students, and contains many different parts including giving an oral presentation in front of evaluators who do not give out the topic ahead of time. If students fail this exam, they have to go through another year of high school and try again the following year.

One of the major problems in this system has been the fact that students are relatively young when they need to decide what careers they want. If they start a literature program, for example, and want to go into education, and then later decide that they would prefer to be scientists

instead and do scientific research, it is very hard to switch
programs.

77)	Learn what grade your kid is in or what grade you are in.

French schools are organized differently than American
schools, which go from kindergarten to 12th grade. In
France, if you send your child to a Parisian school or if
you yourself are in school, you will see that schools start
with "la maternelle" – nursery school – before elementary
school. Most children go to nursery school for two years
and then enter into "CP" – cours préparatoire – which is
the first level, the equivalent of 1st grade in the U.S. The
next level is CE1 (cours élémentaire 1) and CE2 (cours
élémentaire 2), the equivalent of 2nd and 3rd grade in the
U.S. Then you go to CM1 (cours moyen 1) and CM2 (cours
moyen 2) which are 4th and 5th grade in the U.S. Then you
have "collège" which is Middle School, which is 6ème,
5ème and 4ème and 3ème (6th, 7th and 8th and 9th grade).
Then you have your "lycée" – high school – with seconde,
premier and terminale (10th, 11th and 12th grades).

78)	Be happy to be paid 13 times a year.

Some French companies pay their employees thirteen
times a year. Usually employees are paid per month, so if
you work for a French company and start looking for your
paycheck after two weeks like in the U.S., you are going
to have to wait a little longer. If you are the type of person
who lives from paycheck to paycheck, you will have to do
some rearranging and manage your money differently.

"Le treizième mois" – this thirteenth payment of salary
– is usually paid at the end of the year but it can
sometimes be divided up into two or three payments at
different times of the year. It is like a bonus and there

may be specific conditions you have to fulfill to get it, but if it is part of your contract when a French company hires you, you will normally be receiving it.

In recent years, French companies have started withholding part of employees' pay for income tax just like U.S. companies do with their employees, but this practice is something relatively new to the country. January is when you need to file your income taxes in France.

If you work for a French company, you will come under the work regulations for the company. If you have an office job, you will work only 35 hours a week. You will also be entitled to 5 weeks of vacation after only one year on the job, so unlike the U.S., where you have only two weeks off until you work for the same company for five years, and then you get only a third week off until you work at the same place for ten years and if you are lucky to be with the same company for ten years and if that same company is still around after all this time, you may get four weeks off every year. Just like in the U.S., there is a minimum wage that is adjusted regularly to take into consideration inflation.

| 79) | Take care of your teeth. |

Go to the dentist and take care of your teeth, because dental care is part of the French health system and is covered by Social Security if you are enrolled in their program through work or marriage or maybe even school. Note, however, that dentists in France go to dental school and not medical school. It is considered a different branch, so unlike dentists in the U.S. who have to go through medical school first, French dentists go directly through dental school.

When I was a student, I didn't have this coverage and I needed to get two wisdom teeth removed, so I went to the dental school and volunteered to be a guinea pig. I must have been crazy, but I was young then and young people sometimes do crazy things. I did have my two teeth removed successfully but there were about twenty students standing around, observing the operation. I must admit that I almost fainted, though, when I returned and had the sutures removed. Once again, there were lots of students standing around so there were at least a few with some revival skills.

80)	Visit a "maison de campagne."

Parisians love Paris but they also love to leave Paris whenever they get the chance. Some have a country home – une "maison de campagne" - that is usually not very far from Paris where they can go to for weekends and eventually for vacations if they are not heading down South like the greater majority of Parisians in the summertime. It is a chance to get away from city life, even though life in Paris does not seem like city life compared to other major cities. In fact, many people think Paris is actually a big village, maybe because it is divided up into twenty districts that have their own distinct "ambiance." The fact that there are no skyscrapers within the city limits could also add to the impression that you are not in a metropolis. Parisians, however, still like to get away from the traffic and the crowds and enjoy peaceful moments out in the countryside.

If you become friends with someone who has a country home and they invite you to join them, by all means do so. You will undoubtedly find a small stone house of some sort surrounded by the usual walls you find around French homes. Once you get outside of Paris, you will find that people are going about their lives at a more casual pace. Many of the country roads are lined with trees dating back to the times of kings, but you will not see grass lawns like you do in the U.S. Behind those stone walls, you will basically find stone and dirt driveways and not much else. If the country house is more recent, maybe you will have a piece of lawn and the house may be a little more modern, but it is not as common as the old stone ones.

| 81) | Take a break from the city. |

Most Parisians think that the only place to live in France is Paris, but there are many other interesting locations to visit and access to these towns and villages is very easy, especially with the excellent train system that exists in France. You can take a train to practically any town in France from Paris, and places like Versailles and St.-Germain-en-Laye are not far and accessible by train or RER. To the East, you have Disneyland Paris if you are homesick for Mickey and Minnie Mouse. If you want to go as far as London, you also have the Eurostar that will take you under the English Channel to England in just a few hours.

The "TGV" – train à grande vitesse – is a high-speed train that can whisk you away from Paris and take you to other cities in France in just a few hours.

| 82) | Find a nanny if you need one. |

If you work and need to find someone to watch your child or children during your working hours, you have several options. You can try to enroll your children in a "crèche" – day care - if they are still infants, but you usually have to enroll them a long time ahead of time. You can put them in "l'école maternelle" – nursery school – if they are a little older.

You can also get a list of "assistantes maternelles" – nannies – online. These ladies are registered with the town hall and go through medical exams to be sure they are in good health and have no illnesses that are contagious. You will need to call the nanny and find out what her daily or monthly rates are, and then you will need to draw up a contract with her. In France, they love contracts, but contracts provide everything in writing and make all the details very clear. Your nanny will be like your employee and she will be entitled to paid time off too. Your nanny is allowed to watch up to three children along with her own children and will provide her services in her own home, so you will need to drop your child or children off at her place and then pick them up at the end of the day.

Some Parisians prefer to hire a nanny "au pair" and have her live with them and watch over their children in their own homes if they can afford to do so. In this case, you would have to provide room and board in exchange for the services of a young girl who is often not French. These girls watch and take care of the children and sometimes do some light housekeeping. Many "au pair" girls come to Paris for a limited time, maybe a year or two, to work and most of the time to learn the language.

If you are looking for someone for more than one year, you would probably be better off looking for an "assistante maternelle" and taking your children back and forth to her place. Most "assistantes maternelles" usually provide their services for years, the time it takes for your kids to grow up. They are usually mothers themselves and therefore have lots of experience in caring for children.

| 83) | Buy your ticket before you get on the train. |

The train company in France is called "la SNCF" (Société nationale de chemins de fer) and you will see signs indicating where your nearest train station is located.

If you don't opt for a monthly or weekly or daily transportation card or if you are traveling beyond the zones for a card you have purchased, you will need to buy a train ticket before you get on the train, because unlike in the U.S., conductors do not sell tickets on the train. You occasionally have "un contrôleur" – someone who checks your ticket to see that you have validated it in a machine you need to use before you get on the train. If you do not have a ticket or a validated ticket, this gentleman will give you a fine – "une amende." They are not always on the train too. Sometimes they will be waiting at the exits of train stations, so be sure to hold on to your ticket.

Trains are very popular in France and are generally pretty much on time. There are several major train stations in Paris: la gare St. Lazare, la gare du Nord, la gare de l'Est, la gare d'Austerlitz and la gare de Lyon, which are the oldest train stations, and you also have the more recent stations of la gare Montparnasse and la gare de Bercy. Most of the trains are now modern and comfortable.

I have already mentioned the TGV, which is one of the fastest trains in the world, which can take you from Paris to several different destinations in France in no time.

You can also take a train from Paris if you want to go to London, just to name one of many cities in other countries you can go to directly from Paris. Years ago, you had take a boat to get to England and use the ferry for your car if you were driving, but now you can go right under the English Channel on the Eurostar.

84)	Try some crêpes.

If you have never tried a French crêpe, this is the time to do so. It will make your day. There are wonderful crêperies in Paris, and there are even some neighborhoods, like the Latin Quarter, where you can buy a hot crêpe right off the round griddle, covered with sugar and butter, or chocolate, just to name a couple of fillings that are typically offered. In restaurants, you will find a wider choice than at the stands in the street, and in a creperie, most of which are run by people from the province of Brittany (la Bretagne, in French), you will also be able to purchase some nice cider that goes perfectly with your crêpe.

85)	Don't be surprised by meager French wardrobes.

One thing that Americans have, especially American women, is a whole closet full of clothes and shoes of all kinds. Some people have so many clothes they cannot even close their closet doors.

Most Parisians I knew did not have these over-stuffed closets. In fact, one of my first roommates from years ago had all of three dresses, two pairs of shoes and a coat, all worth a small fortune. Some people will sacrifice quantity for quality, especially in Paris where the cost of clothing and everything else can be notoriously high. They tend to buy a few basic pieces of clothing and a few accessories that they add to change their appearance.

Styles, of course, change, but generally speaking, I have the impression that clothing is more fitted in France than in the U.S. I could always tell a French blouse from an American one, because there would be a couple of seams down the back to make it more shapely.

86)	Don't walk on the grass in public parks.

Those beautiful lawns you see in the public parks like the Luxembourg Garden or the Tuileries in Paris are for show only. Do not be tempted to walk on the grass or lie down on it. There are signs everywhere saying "Pelouse interdite" which means "Forbidden Lawn" – in other words, do not walk on the grass.

| 87) | Stand to the right on escalators in public areas. |

Parisians are always in a hurry, so move out of the way and let them go by. They will race up escalators, slide their transportation tickets into the automatic control machines at the entrances of public transportation and rush through the turnstiles and head towards their subways or trains. They will become annoyed if you stand to the left on the escalator and slow them down. You are supposed to stand to the right if you yourself are not rushing up the stairs and outrunning everybody else.

| 88) | Pay the price you see. |

Prices for clothes and food already include the hefty VAT tax, or sales tax, you have to pay, so you will not be adding anything on to the prices you see. The prices will be high enough already.

You should note that there are clothing sales – "les soldes" - twice a year in Paris, towards the end of January and the end of June for two weeks. In the U.S., we are used to seeing sales all the time, for just about every holiday, but in Paris, you are going to find sales only twice a year.

| 89) | Be an individual. |

A lot of Americans like to join organizations, be a member of a club or a group and to go along with whatever everybody else does. Community service is very popular in the U.S., but it is not the case in France. Aside from maybe some sort of religious affiliation, most French people are not group-oriented. You can even see it in their politics with so many different political parties with different ways of thinking that not one single party ever has the majority, and elections are conducted in two phases, to group together similarly-thinking parties to try to get a majority. It is said that there are as many French groups as there are individuals in France.

90)	Don't get yelled at at an open market.

When you go to open markets which take place two or three times a week, do not help yourself to whatever is displayed. You are supposed to tell the sales person what you want and the quantity you want and this person will put the items in a paper bag and weigh them. I made the mistake years ago of picking out an apple that I wanted and I almost got my hand slapped. I must say I never returned to that stand ever again, but I didn't yet know that I was doing something you are not supposed to do. If you are in a supermarket like Carrefour, Auchan, Leclerc and Casino, then you can help yourself, but not when you go to the market or a fruit and vegetable stand.

Open markets are wonderful places and some of them seem very lively since certain vendors will call out what they are selling or draw customers to their stands in other ways. I used to buy delicious candy at a candy stand in the suburban town of Puteaux where a lady always called out, "Goûte! Goûte!" (literally meaning "taste (this)"). You could hear her fifty feet away.

91)	Know how to use your fork and knife.

You may not know this, but there is even etiquette for eating salad in France. You never cut the lettuce in the bowl or on the plate in front of you. You are supposed to fold the leaf onto the fork with the help of your knife and then eat the whole leaf.

You may see some Parisians using a knife and fork to

eat their pizza as well. Most Americans are not going to waste any time cutting up their slice of pizza, but they do it in France.

92)	Check store hours.

Many stores in Paris do not stay open as late as stores in the U.S. Some close as early as 7 p.m., so if you are planning on going shopping at night, you need to check out store hours first. Most stores are also closed on Sunday, not by choice but by law, but the government has become more flexible in recent years, especially since the tourist trade in Paris builds the economy, and you will find some open on Sundays.

93)	Try a different cheese every day.

I hope you are a cheese lover because you are going to the ultimate country of cheese. The most popular ones are camembert, chèvre, emmenthal, roquefort and brie just to name a very few. There are so many types of cheese in France that you could eat a different kind every day for a full year. Cheese spreads like Boursin are also very popular.

I also recommend trying "petit suisse" – which is a smooth and creamy cube-shaped cheese that is like thick yogurt that you take out of the container and mix with some sugar before you eat it. Délicieux!

If you have the chance, you should try a "raclette." This is a type of French fondue consisting of melted cheese and bread, and sometimes boiled potatoes are served as well. Originating in Switzerland, this dish made its way into the French Alps during the Middle Ages and is very popular in France. A machine melts your cheese and you scrape it off and coat your bread and potatoes with it.

If you are not a cheese expert but you like cheese, you

will probably become a "connaisseur" during your stay in Paris. You will know how to open a box of camembert and press your finger on it to see if it is soft enough – assez moelleux – for you. The gooier the camembert, the better it is.

94)	Learn to eat yogurt.

Yogurt is popular in France and you will find a wide variety, from plain to flavored. There are even machines you can buy if you want to make your own. French people will sometimes have yogurt instead of cheese for the cheese phase of their meal. Danone and Yoplait, which you can find even in the U.S., are probably the producers of the most popular types of yogurt in France.

95)	Be a tourist and ignore what Parisians do.

Many Parisians have never been up the Eiffel Tower. Some have never stepped foot in Napoleon's Tomb. A lot of them never go to l'Opéra or spend any time in the Louvre. The places which draw the most tourists in Paris are places that most Parisians avoid and they do not know what they are missing. Maybe they see these monuments every day, and they are just every day places to them, or maybe they don't want to be with groups of tourists, but you should not do like the Parisians do. You should take the time to visit all the wonderful monuments and museums Paris has to offer. Stroll down the Champs-Elysées – it's the most beautiful street in the world and it's free. Take pictures of Concorde Square with its beautiful fountains and marvelous statues. Take a look inside l'Opéra and even go to a ballet or an opera when they are open. Visit the oldest theater in Paris, la Comédie Française which was created by Louis XIV. Buy clothes and souvenirs and perfume at Galeries Lafayette or

Printemps, two large department stores not far from gare St. Lazare. Gawk at the designer boutiques along Faubourg St. Honoré. Take a walk in the Tuilerie Gardens and spend days at the Louvre. Browse the old book stands along the Seine River – les bouquinistes – with their stands that they open up during the day for customers and close at night. Visit Notre-Dame cathedral, even though part of the original structure was destroyed in a fire and rebuilt. Take a walk through the Latin Quarter, so called because it was here that professors during the Middle Ages stood in the streets with their students and gave their classes in Latin. Have coffee (if you can afford it) in some of the most famous cafés, like La Coupole or Les Deux Magots. Go inside the Sorbonne and see the old medieval tapestries and the wooden lecture halls dating back to the 13th century. Take a walk back in time and stroll along cobblestone streets where pilgrims walked centuries ago. Visit Luxembourg Garden where kids love to sail little boats in the huge fountain. Visit Chinatown in the 13th arrondissement, where Asians from former French colonies have settled and set up restaurants and businesses. Go to Montmartre and check out Sacré-Coeur and see a wonderful panoramic view of the city from the hilltop and stairways. Get your portrait drawn at the square in Montmartre where all the artists are. Visit Napoleon's tomb and imagine Napoleon inside all seven coffins that enclose him. Take pictures of the beautiful fountains at Trocadéro across from the Eiffel Tower. And yes, go up that Eiffel Tower, because you will see a fabulous view of the entire city, and there is even a restaurant where you can have lunch or dinner after making appropriate reservations. Get out and be a tourist and take as many pictures as you want. They will turn out to be wonderful memories for you if you don't end up staying forever in Paris.

| 96) | Find your way around courtyards. |

When you go into the entrance of some of the older
apartment buildings, there is a courtyard with several
entrances to different apartments. The concierge will
guide you to wherever you need to go if you are unfamiliar
with the place. Similarly, old schools also have courtyards
where children can play during their "récréation" – recess
from classes.

| 97) | Save money on college tuition. |

If you are a student who took the bac or if you are a
parent whose child or children went through the French
school system and passed the baccalauréat, you have just
saved a lot of money if you or your children plan to go to
college in France. Depending on what field you or your
children want to go into, there are many French
universities for which you will pay just a minimal
registration fee. There are, of course, private institutions
that cost money, but if you go to a college subsidized by
the government, you will not be paying tuition. Some
requirements for professions, however, can vary from one
country to another and certain degrees may be valid for
one country but not for another. If you plan to become a
doctor, lawyer, architect or educator, for example, just to
name a few, you would have to decide if you are going to
stay in France or come back to your own country and plan
your education and career accordingly.

What I do recommend is that you get your degree or
degrees in your field of interest and learn and perfect your
French language skills at the same time, unless you plan
to specialize in languages to become an interpreter,
translator or teacher. There are many international
opportunities and companies are always looking for
people who speak other languages. If you are specialized
in a certain field and have language skills as well, more

doors will be open to you.

98)	Watch your budget.

If you were not living in a city before going to Paris, you may find that you will be paying a lot more money than you were in the U.S. If you rent, depending on where you live and what type of housing you have, your rent will always be exorbitant, especially if you live inside the city limits. Water tends to be very expensive, and I had many friends who even purchased hand-held showerheads that you could turn on and off easily to save on water. Electricity costs much more, which is why you have hallways with a timer that turns the light off automatically after a certain amount of time; you have to keep pushing a button to turn it back on if you are waiting in a hallway somewhere. There is a tax on televisions that you have to pay every year. If you live in an apartment, which is most likely the case if you live in Paris, you will have HOA fees – "les charges" – to pay for the elevator, the upkeep of any grass or shrubs on the property and the salary for the concierge. Your grocery bills will be much higher than what you were used to paying in the U.S. If you decide to buy an apartment in Paris, you will have to pay property taxes and not only the HOA fees but any renovations the home owners' association may vote on to maintain the building in good condition.

I knew many Parisians who were working and yet had to watch out for every little expense. They turned down the heat, practically measured every glass of water they used, didn't buy as much meat and looked for drastic means to cut back on everything. If you have lots of money, Paris is a wonderful place, but if you do not have a lot of money and have to watch your expenses, Paris could be a hard place for you to live in. Maybe this is true of many major cities, but it is especially true for Paris.

| 99) | Learn to talk about politics. |

One of the most popular topics of discussion in France is politics. Everyone seems to be constantly talking about all the different parties and whatever measures the government happens to be taking, and there are many parties, from the far right to extreme left, with no one single party having the majority. Over the years, French television programs have made fun of countless politicians.

France is also part of the European Union, which widens even further political topics to discuss. Citizens of the European Union can live and work in other member countries without going through the process of obtaining work permits. France's relationships with other member countries have been strengthened through this political and economic organization.

Many French people are concerned about the way their country is run and do not hesitate to voice their opinions during strikes or demonstrations. Over the years, they called for reforms by the government in a wide range of activities, from wages to educational system reforms to pension restructuring to agricultural support. Some professions, such as farming and trucking, have been directly affected by agreements with the European Union, and in the past, there have been a number of actions, such as slow-moving trucks blocking major highways and farm products dumped in roads, to express disagreement with what was being done.

| 100) | Forget your diet and go to the pastry shop. |

French pastries will help you get through even the toughest of days. Paris has pastry shops everywhere throughout the city, and in all of France there are around 30,000 bakeries. If you are a dessert lover, this is your chance to find the best pastries ever, from the "religieuse"

– a stacked cream puff coated with delectable frosting – to the "tarte au citron" – wonderfully tangy lemon tart – to the "baba au rhum" – a scrumptious rum cake drenched in rum, just to name a few. The list of pastries to try goes on: écairs, crème brûlé, mousse au chocolat, crème caramel, clafoutis which is a delicious cake with fruit in it, madeleines, tartes aux pommes with apples, tarte aux fraises with strawberries. In fact, there are around 40 different pastries you can try, and all of them will have you returning for more. The pies – les tartes – never have a crust over them like in the U.S., and all the fruit that is marvelously arranged with make your mouth water.

Many of these pastries are consumed during your "goûter" – that 4 o'clock tea that everybody likes to have. You can savor them along with a cup of tea or coffee.

Some pastries are very complicated to make and require years of skills and practice to achieve the level of excellence you will find in pastries from pastry shops, but others are easier to make and you can even try to bake some yourself. You have a simple "quatre quarts," for example, which is a pound cake with equal portions of four ingredients as the name indicates. You can also try making a "tarte tatin" which is a caramelized apple pie that you bake upside down. If you want to give it a try, you can find many easy recipes online.

What you will not find in pastry shops are cookies in packages. You can go to the supermarket or local grocery store and find packaged cookies like you do in the U.S., although the cookies that are popular in France are not like the cookies you find in the U.S. The most popular cookies are butter cookies or cookies with chocolate on top of them called "Petits Ecoliers." Cookies called "palmiers" are popular as well as macarons, madeleines and meringues.

| 101) | Close your shutters at night. |

In the U.S., most homes have curtains and when you want some privacy at night or when you want less sunshine during the day, you will pull your curtains. In France, particularly in Paris, you are going to have shutters on your windows that you will close up at night and sometimes when you are absent from your home for an extended time. You will have to open your window and pull them shut and then latch them so they are locked. If you don't have small window shutters, you will have a roll-down shutter called "des stores," for your balcony or patio, just like they have in stores.

| 102) | Check your check. |

In many restaurants, the tip is automatically included and your check will show you if that is the case or not. It is not uncommon to include the service charge and it will say "service compris." If you are happy with the service, you can always leave a little extra. If you are not happy with the service, no, you cannot get your service charge back. If the service was bad, I'd say don't go back there the next time.

| 103)) | Take the RER to cross Paris fast. |

If you need to get across the city, from one end to the other, use the RER, which is the express train, and not the subway. The subway stops at all types of stations and takes longer for that reason. The RER will get you to your destination in no time.

Before this system was completed years ago, it would take almost two hours to cross the city, because there was no direct connection, but with the completion of the express train system, Parisians can go from one end to the other and even beyond to nearby suburbs in approximately 30 minutes.

104)	Spend a day at the zoo.

There is a zoo to the East of Paris, the Vincennes Zoo, which is located in the Bois de Vincennes. If you like animals and want a change of pace, you can walk through the zoo and see all types of animals. Get your walking shoes out because there are 36 acres to visit. This zoo was created in 1934 and has about 2,000 animals, reptiles and fish and 180 different species. The zoo was renovated a number of years ago and is now open.

105)	Don't bother looking for Dollar Shops.

In the U.S., we have several chains of dollar shops, stores in which you pay one dollar for everything in the store or shops which sell all kinds of items for just a few dollars. There are no dollar shops in Paris, or even euro shops. You do have some discount stores but you are not going to find anything like a dollar shop that you have in the U.S. There are some large chain stores like Auchan and Carrefour and Monoprix which sell both food and a variety of other items at prices that are lower than specialty shops or your local corner "épicerie," but they tend to be like Walmart or Target here in the U.S. and do not sell everything for the same price, like dollar shops do.

106)	Drink bottled water.

Most Parisians do not drink the water from their

faucets and use the water they have in their apartments for cleaning, washing clothes or taking showers or baths. Although some people claim that you can drink water from the tap, many still have doubts about how healthy it actually is. You can ask for tap water in restaurants, if you want, but there still seems to be a trend to order mineral water in a bottle. Most Parisians purchase drinking water in bottles at the supermarket or local "épicerie" – the corner grocery store.

If you are a health enthusiast or if you have some health issue such as the notorious "mal au foie" (liver issues) that considerable numbers of French people are constantly complaining about, you can do some research on what type of mineral water could improve your condition and you can look into going outside Paris, to towns that are spas. Many years ago, I happened to be a student in Vichy and spent a summer in this town, which is known for its mineral water and health benefits. All types of people were walking around with water bottles around their necks because they had access to fountains as part of their treatment or "cure" as they say in French. You don't always have to go to the spa to drink the mineral water since you can buy most of the different types of mineral water in bottles, but many of the spas offer baths and shower treatments for which you would have to go to their location.

107)	Relax and buy some French perfume or cologne.

If you are a woman, you will be in perfume heaven, and if you are a man, you will have all kinds of colognes to choose from. If you like designer brands, your perfume or cologne will be pricey, but your enjoyment will be immense. Some of the more famous perfume producers are Guerlain, Chanel, Yves Saint-Laurent, Cartier and Dior.

I remember walking into the Guerlain shop on the Champs-Elysées years ago. This store is still there for you to discover. I remember my first favorite of the time, a perfume called "Heure bleue" that I purchased in a beautifully decorated metal spray decanter. "Shalimar" is one of their perfumes that can often be found in the U.S. Later I discovered others that many people like as well, such as Chanel no. 5 and Opium by Yves St. Laurent. The French know how to make their perfumes and colognes, so check them out. In some stores, like Galeries Lafayettes or Printemps, they will sometimes spray a little on your wrist so you can get a whiff of what it smells like. Enjoy!

If you have a gift for detecting and mixing fragrances, you could even become a "nose" for a perfume company. These people are the experts that can detect a fragrance and break it down into its basic elements. However, if you want to try to get into this profession, you have to first of all have "the nose" that can make distinctions in fragrances, and it generally takes about four years to become "a nose," because you have to learn to distinguish between approximately 1500 different scents.

| 108) | Don't expect ice with your soda in a café. |

If you go to a café, they will not put ice in your soda. You have to ask for it and they will give it to you separately, in a bowl, so that you can add however much you want. With the price you will be paying for a glass of soda in a café, you will be glad not to have your glass filled with ice and not your drink. However, if you go to a fast food place, you will get your ice.

| 109) | Try a croque monsieur in a café. |

There is a special sandwich you will find only in cafés.

It is a grilled ham and cheese sandwich on two slices of regular bread like we have in the U.S., what is called "pain de mie" in France. There is also another sandwich called croque madame, which is the same sandwich with a poached egg on the top. The egg on top is supposed to make you think of a woman's hat and is how this particular sandwich got its name, but you may have to use your imagination a little when you see it. That egg on top never did look like a hat to me.

110)	Know your time zones

If you have relatives and friends that you want to call on the east coast of the U.S., there will generally be six hours of time difference. Paris will be six hours ahead of the time in the U.S., so if it's four in the afternoon in Paris, it is only ten in the morning on the east coast. If it is ten in the morning in Paris, a perfect time to make a phone call, keep in mind that it is only four in the morning in New York. If, of course, you are calling someone in the mid-west or on the west coast, you are going to add on hour differences according to what time zone they are in.

You might also want to note that France does not do daylight savings time on the same date as the U.S. There will be a couple of weeks of odd time differences in the year because of this. For example, in 2021, French time is supposed to spring ahead one hour on March 28, 2021, but in the U.S., unless some change is voted in the meantime, it springs ahead on March 14, 2021, so during those two weeks, there is five hours' difference on the east coast with France and not six hours. French time is going to fall back on October 31, 2021 whereas the U.S. is going to wait another week before doing so, so during that week, there is a difference of five hours again, but only for a week this time. Daylight savings time has been a topic of discussion for some years now, so who knows what the future will hold, but in the past, it has always been a little complicated when countries don't change time at the same time.

| 111) | Leave your hotel key at the reception desk. |

If you happen to be staying in a hotel for a while, you will normally have a big key with a clunky key chain on it. Unlike in the U.S., you will be leaving the key at the reception desk whenever you go out and getting it back from the reception desk when you return to your room. In any case, you will undoubtedly remember to leave your key, because if you try to stick it in your pocket, you will have a big, bulging pocket and if you are a woman with a purse and your purse is not very big, you probably would not even be able to close your bag. Just leave it at the reception desk.

| 112) | Find out if you have a private bathroom at your hotel. |

If you are going to a hotel that is not expensive, you should check to see if you have a private bathroom or not ("une salle de bains privée," because some less expensive hotels often have one bathroom that is shared by everyone on one floor. If this is the case of your hotel, in most instances, you will have to pick up the key to the bathroom when you want to take a shower or a bath. If you do not want to use a common bathroom, you should choose another hotel and maybe pay a little more for your room. Be sure to ask about it whenever you make a hotel reservation.

| 113) | Watch documentaries on French TV. |

Being in Paris and having the possibility to actually visit different places, you will come to appreciate many documentaries you may see on French television about the City of Light as well as other places you could visit. You can also learn about subjects you may not have known much about. You will learn a lot just by watching TV in France, and they know how to create very interesting documentaries. Certain French movies may be hard to figure out, but French documentaries are outstanding. You will be able to see programs that discuss not only topics and events happening in Paris, but also present all types of interesting information about other towns or topics that may be controversial. "Des racines et des ailes" has been around for 19 seasons and is a way of discovering the historical side of different places in France. Years ago, Jacques Cousteau did underwater explorations and documented many of his discoveries, and even though you may not see his documentaries on TV anymore, you can find them online. "Thalassa" is a program about oceans and sea life and has been around since 1975. "Envoyé special" is another program where journalists interview different people and discuss current issues. These are just a few, but they are worth your time and they will help you learn French as well.

| 114) | Do something unusual. |

You may think that it is weird to visit catacombs and see all kinds of skulls, but you can actually go on a tour of the catacombs in Paris. Under Paris, there is a tunnel that holds the remains of almost six million people.

You may have read "Les Misérables" or seen the musical, or maybe you read or have seen "Le fantôme de l'Opéra," (The Phantom of the Opera) both of which have scenes in the sewers of Paris. Years ago, you could get on a boat and float around in the "égouts" that are all underground, but in more recent years, you can only go down and see information about the system and catch a glimpse of the canals that flow under the city.

If you are a fan of cemeteries, you can go to Père Lachaise cemetery where many famous writes and some celebrities are buried.

Not every city has boats that can take you for a tour of the city on the river. Paris has its "bateaux mouches" – boats which will take you down the river and around the île de la Cité where Notre Dame cathedral is located.

If you have the chance, go to a show called "Son et Lumière." I went to one at Ecole militaire next to Napoleon's Tomb one year when my sister was visiting. We rushed to get to the show on time and took a cab that weaved its way through traffic along the Champs-Elysees, and I never saw my sister's face turn so white. We got to the Ecole militaire and ran up the cobblestone pathway in our heels to the large door. For this particular show, there were only a few people and a few chairs, but "Son et Lumière" shows are light shows with music and someone talking about the history of whatever you are looking at. Years ago, I saw spectacular shows at Versailles where there were even fireworks and people in costumes with horses and carriages. You will never see anything like this elsewhere, so go to one, even if some are more spectacular than others. It will be worth your while.

Paris is full of all kinds of unusual places. With time, new ones appear and old ones sometimes disappear. Years ago, near la Madeleine in the center of the city, there was a café with an indoor zoo and even a lion behind a glass cage. The café went out of business, but it was a very unusual experience. It's not every day in Paris that you see a lion staring at you, face to face with you, while you're drinking your coffee.

115)	Go to the American Consulate if you need help.

If you are American and if, for example, you lose your passport or have legal questions about staying in Paris, the American Consulate is there to help. The U.S. Consulate and the U.S. Embassy are located near Place de la Concorde, and you can get to them easily.

If you are a U.S. citizen and your spouse is not a French citizen either, and if you have children in France, you will need to register them as U.S. citizens born abroad at the Embassy. Unlike the U.S., children in France born of parents who are not French do not automatically obtain French nationality. Laws regarding double nationality with American citizenship change over time, so you will need to check with the current situation. Before I went to France, there was a time when Americans living in France could have double nationality, but when I was living there, this was no longer a possibility, and I retained my U.S. citizenship and obtained resident permits to live in France. My son who was born and raised in France is a U.S. citizen born abroad in the eyes of the French government, and unless laws change, he would not have double nationality. The U.S. embassy is the place where you will find answers to your questions about nationality.

116)	Use your commute time wisely.

Once you have become accustomed to Paris, you will probably have some sort of routine or commute back and forth, maybe to work or to school. Your life as a new arrival will eventually become your life as an "old hand" or "vieux routier" as the French say. Your surroundings eventually become so familiar to you that you don't really notice anything new about them after a while. Parisians in the trains or subways and even on the buses will read or knit or spend the time talking with friends or colleagues who travel the same route or looking at their phones or laptop computers.

Many years ago, I commuted from Puteaux to Paris by taking the train that goes into gare St. Lazare. I'd see the same people every day at the train station. A group of three women loved to chat all the way into the city, which was about a 15-minute ride. Other people would pull out newspapers or books. I don't know how many books I read during the years I commuted into the city, but it turned out to be quite a few.

From gare St. Lazare, I'd take the subway, and of course, this was during rush hour with hundreds of people hurrying to get to work. At the time, which was many years ago, I wore hard contact lenses because the soft lenses were not invented yet. You would wear hard contacts like you wear glasses, and order a new pair maybe once every two years. I was, of course, rushing to get to work in the entrance to the subway when all of a sudden, I realized I was not seeing as well as I should. I had lost one of my lenses. Of all places to lose a contact lens, it had to be during rush hour at the entrance of one of the busiest métro stations in the city. I looked at all the people walking through the tunnel and started looking desperately at the floor. Before I knew it, I had all kinds of people looking around on the floor as well. Maybe they thought I was looking for lost money or gold. Maybe they thought there was something unusual about the floor. A few people did ask what I was searching for, and when I told them, they'd shake their heads and give me that sad or sometimes amused, "good luck" look. I never did find the contact lens, and it was probably totally pulverized by all the people walking by, but I still remember everyone looking around at the floor and half the time not even knowing what they were looking for. Don't you just love city life.

| 117) | Get to the airport early. |

There are two major airports near Paris and a third one that is more for private planes. You have Roissy Charles de Gaulle Airport to the North and Orly Airport to the South. Le Bourget is the third, smaller airport. Roissy and Orly can be reached easily using public transportation or shuttles that go between the city and the airport. You can, of course, take a cab, but it will cost you more in this case. Like all major cities, there is always traffic, so when you are planning to take a plane from one of these airports, you need to give yourself plenty of time to get there. If you are in a real hurry, a cab driver would probably find a way to get you there in no time. There are cab stations everywhere in Paris and at least during the daytime, you can usually find cab drivers waiting for customers. As is the case in most major airports in the world, you will need to be at the airport at least two hours ahead of time, if not more, to check in and go through all the controls before you board the plane.

| 118) | Get some cartes de visite. |

Cartes de visite – visiting cards – are still very popular in Paris and throughout France. American business people are used to having cards with their company name, their name and title and contact information for business meetings, but Parisians will have cards on hand to give to you with just their personal address and contact information. Sometimes they will use this card to send you some type of greeting or message or to invite you to some event or party they may be organizing. It is also used when you have just met someone and they want to give you their phone number or address. Instead of searching for a pen or paper, you can just whip out your own card and exchange cards with the other person.

| 119) | Enjoy French technology. |

France was one of the first countries to have the beginnings of what later developed into the World Wide Web and the Internet. Back in the 1980's, they came out with a telephone system called the Minitel, which allowed you to access phone numbers and other basic information directly through the phone.

An advantage you have by being in Paris is that you will have access to Wi Fi and all the latest technology, so you will be able to continue to keep in touch with old friends and family as well as what is going on elsewhere in the world. Technology has changed the world and made it a much smaller place. Years ago, when I first moved to France, there was no easy way to communicate other than by phone, and phone calls were so expensive back then, that you had to make your calls short and to the point only on special occasions. This is no longer the case, and you can check with your phone provider for special international rates if you plan on calling home or will not be using the Internet to talk with your family and friends outside of Paris.

If you are interested in science and technology, there is a wonderful science museum at Porte de la Villette called Cité des Sciences et de l'Industrie. It is actually the largest science museum in all of Europe, so if you want to check out this museum, you can get there easily.

You may decide to buy a computer in France. If you do buy a French computer, note that you will have a French keyboard. I myself learned to type on a French keyboard, so when I write in French, I do not have to go to codes or tables to insert the accents. The advantage of using a French keyboard is to be able to type text in both English and French. The location of letters, however, is different on the two keyboards: the French keyboard is called an AZERTY keyboard and the English keyboard is a QWERTY keyboard. If you have a hard time with the French keyboard or are writing only in English and do not need the accents, you can usually change the language setting on a computer to give you the English keyboard, but you will not see it physically in front of you. If you are a touch typist and do not look at the keyboard when you type, you will not have any problem, but if you are not a touch typist, you can always print out a copy of the English keyboard and refer to it when you are typing.

120)	Discover the world of art.

Art will be around you every day and you will have access to museums and temporarily exhibits that will allow you to see all types of artwork. It is a wonderful opportunity for you to learn more about artists and artwork, so take advantage of it.

I myself used to go to many of the temporary exhibits they had at the Grand Palais, which is located down the street from the Arch of Triumph and towards la Place de la Concorde. You can go to Quai d'Orsay, which was a train station that was changed into an art museum many years ago. Visit l'Orangerie in the Tuilerie Gardens and spend days at the Louvre, just to name a few.

121)	Walk through history.

Needless to say, walking through Paris is like walking through history. Parisians have made great efforts to preserve the traces of their history and rightfully so. Technology has opened doors to information about whatever you may be interested in, so whenever you see something you are curious about, look it up, find out its history and how it came to be in Paris. The Arch of Triumph was built by Napoleon to commemorate his victories. It took two hundred years to build Notre Dame and when the cathedral builders disappeared, the secret of how to build cathedrals was lost forever. The Sorbonne goes back to the middle ages, and before they built a building, courses were given in Latin in the streets, which is why this area of the city is called the Latin Quarter. The Louvre was where kings lived until Louis XIV decided to build a magnificent palace in Versailles to impress the rest of the world and show how powerful he was. The Eiffel Tower was built for a World's Fair in 1889 and was supposed to be a temporary structure. These are just a few examples of all types of history and interesting facts you can find about Paris. History comes to life when you are in Paris.

You can even go to the Comédie Française in the heart of Paris. This theater was created by Louis XIV to promote the development of the arts in France, and classic plays can still be seen here. You can imagine yourself back in time, watching plays that were being presented in the 17th century.

122)	Read French literature and expand your imagination.

Once you have mastered the language, you will be able to discover the world of French literature, and even if you have not yet reached the level you need to understand more complicated books and stories, there are many excellent translations of classic literature. When you are in Paris, you are where many of these stories take place. Reading classics will also allow you to discover what life in the City of Light was like during the French Revolution or at the times of Kings and royalty or during the 18th or 19th centuries.

If you are desperate to get ahold of books in English, you will find book stores of different kinds everywhere. WH Smith on rue de Rivoli, opposite the Tuileries Garden, specializes in English language books and has many books that have been translated into English from French. Shakespeare and Company is still around and sells English language books in the Latin Quarter. You should also look at la FNAC which has several stores in Paris. La FNAC is a very popular book store chain that sells all types of books and other items, such as CDs. You can find just about everything you want or need to read at la FNAC.

If you are a student, you can sign up for national libraries in Paris, such as la Bibliothèque Sainte-Geneviève in the Latin Quarter and gain access to a wide collection of books of all kinds.

You can also find many smaller bookstores called "librairies" throughout Paris. Some have been struggling because of the pandemic, but hopefully they will still be around for some time to come.

When I was living in Paris, I noticed that a lot of French novels had no pictures on the cover, only the title of the book and the author, which is very different from American books which usually have some type of picture to draw your attention. Check out some popular French novels.

123)	Don't look for French superheroes.

You will see American movies in Paris, sometimes in English with French subtitles, in which case you will see it listed as "V.O." which means "version originale." You will also see American movies that have been dubbed in French with the designation "V.F." which means "version française," so you will see Superman or Batman speaking French, of course. What you will not see are French superheroes, because these characters have never been part of French culture. French fictional heroes are more along the lines of Tintin or Astérix and Obélix, just to name a couple. Tintin is a cartoon character who is an adventurer that is accompanied by his dog Milou. Astérix is a cartoon character who has all types of adventures with his warrior friends from Gaul during Roman times.

There are movies that have been made based on characters like Tintin or Astérix, but the comic albums seem to be even more popular and are widely read.

| 124) | Don't expect French schools to be like the U.S. |

There has always been a tendency for French schools to be much stricter than American schools. In elementary schools, children already learn how to clearly write out and neatly present ideas. They learn to underline certain words, write neatly and make clear presentations. They start learning math at a very early age and by 6th grade already start algebra. Usually they learn two foreign languages in school, because of their proximity and easy access to other countries and cultures.

Grading in the U.S. is based on A, B, C, D or F or 100 points, but in France, the grades are based on 20 points. Nobody gets 20 points. It's impossible. 19, 18 and 17 are excellent and exceptional. To pass, you have to have at least 10, which is still acceptable. You can't compare the two grading systems by doing simple multiplication, because it doesn't work that way in France. A grade of 13 or 14 is very good in the French system.

Nobody is going to have you take a standardized test either. You will, of course, have different level tests to continue on through a program, but they will all be related to whatever baccalauréat program was chosen. The Bac at the end of the high school years is what counts for everything.

School is for academics in France. There are no clubs or sports at school. In Paris, there are no orange school buses like in the U.S. since most students either walk to school or take public transportation, such as the bus or the métro.

Even the classroom set-up will be different from what you are used to. Students in a French classroom are normally at tables for two people and not individual desks, like in the U.S.

Don't expect to go to a prom in a French school. There aren't any. The same applies for graduation ceremonies. When students take the bac, they look at postings on a bulletin board or a listing to see if they passed or not. They don't do caps and gowns and ceremonies like in the U.S.

125)	Listen to some French music.

In Paris, you will have access to all sorts of concerts, from classical music to pop and the latest techno. Since you are in Paris, you will have the possibility to go to a wide range of concerts and shows, so you can check out what is going on very easily.

Just as in the U.S., there are some singers and musicians who remain all-time favorites despite the passing of time, not only because of their wonderful voices but also the poetic lyrics they sang. Just to name a few, here are some of the singers who are still popular today: Georges Brassens, Edith Piaf, Jacques Brel, Charles Aznavour, Gilbert Bécaud, Françoise Hardy, Sylvie Vartan, Claude François, Johnny Hallyday, Jean-Jacques Goldman, Serge Gainsbourg, Daniel Balavoine, Hugues Aufray, Reynaud, Francis Cabrel, Mireille Mathieu, Mylène Farmer, Michel Sardou. More recent popular singers include Stromae and Zaz, just to mention two.

Nowadays you can find the lyrics online if you are still having difficulty understanding some of the language. This will allow you to read along and listen and better understand and appreciate the poetry or what is being expressed.

Jean-Michel Jarre is another name to keep in mind. He is the son of the famous composer Maurice Jarre who wrote the music for films such as "Lawrence of Arabia," "Doctor Zhivago" and "Mad Max Beyond Thunderdome."

Jean-Michel Jarre is known for his spectacular light shows and electronic and techno music and has performed in a number of shows not only in Paris, but in different cities throughout the world. For New Year's 2021, he did a virtual concert of Notre Dame Cathedral, which was online to ring in the new year with a spectacular light show with the cathedral as a setting. If he happens to be performing somewhere in Paris one day, by all means go and see his show.

| 126) | Eat chocolate and French candy. |

If you have a sweet tooth like I do or even "sweet teeth" like someone in New Orleans told me once, you will find all types of chocolate in Paris, from the cheapest kind you find in supermarkets to the fanciest and most expensive and most unbelievably delicious chocolate in specialty shops. When I first saw French chocolates, I couldn't believe how fancy and ornate they could be. Like some dishes in restaurants, they sometimes even seemed too decorative to eat, but chocolate does not last long when I'm around. Chocolates containing alcohol are popular as well, so if you like chocolate and a shot of alcohol, this will make your day.

You will also have access to specialty candy that is not necessarily made in Paris but is readily available there. One of my favorites is Calissons d'Aix, which are made from candied fruit and almond paste and go back to medieval times in Italy when they found their way into southern France. Haribo gummy bears and Carambar are popular with kids. Nougats are another favorite. You can find glazed chestnuts around Christmas time, and they too are absolutely delicious. You also have fruit-flavored hard candy with a soft inside that melts in your mouth. You have dragées and Bêtises de Cambrai. You will find candy you cannot find elsewhere, from soft caramels to hard candy.

| 127) | Have an ice cream cone during your stroll. |

When the weather is warmer, you will find ice cream cone vendors in different places near the parks. During the daytime, woods and park areas like Bois de Boulogne and Bois de Vincennes are pleasant places to take a stroll while enjoying your ice cream cone, and are good locations to take a jog if you feel you need some exercise. Whenever you go to one of the ice cream cone vendors, don't expect to get the huge ice cream cones you sometimes get in the U.S. and don't expect to pay next to nothing for your ice cream in Paris either. Usually you can get one or two scoops and the cone will be much smaller than what you are used to. But the ice cream is always delicious and you can take it anywhere in the park as you go on a stroll through manicured gardens and past finely trimmed bushes and magnificent flowers. You can enjoy the woods if you happen to be at Bois de Boulogne or Bois de Vincennes. This is another one of the many small pleasures you can enjoy in the City of Light.

| 128) | Take advantage of offers from the comité d'entreprise. |

If you work for a French company that has more than 50 employees, you will have access to your company's comité d'entreprise – a committee that promotes the well-being of the company's employees. The comité d'entreprise offers all sorts of interesting deals, from cheap travel arrangements and tours to discounts in stores. The company I worked for even organized holiday events for the children of employees and would give out toys at company Christmas celebrations. If you are an employee of one of a French company, you should check it out.

129)	Learn to live with the new you.

You may want to dress like the French, talk like the French, eat like the French, go on vacation like the French and live like the French. You may be able to blend in with time, and make new friends and discover new ways of thinking and living. Of course, there will be a new you, because you will have experienced what it's like to have lived in another country, in another culture and especially in Paris. You will have another language under your belt and you will probably start to see everything around you differently than from before. But your old self, your original culture, your original values will still be with you too. You will make friends and maybe see life differently, and maybe you will get to the point that you do not feel you belong anywhere, because you are not French but you are not exactly the same person you were before you discovered what it is to live in Paris.

130)	Discover la joie de vivre.

Fully enjoy and appreciate the French lifestyle. Spend time in the cafés. Take the time to be with those you love. Don't let work stress you out. Take everything in stride and enjoy la plus belle ville du monde.

I always noticed that my French friends were generally happy to be in France and content with their way of life. "On est bien chez nous" – "We're happy at home, in our country" – is an expression that I heard often when I was living in France.

Years ago, a French friend of mine told me she had figured out how to get to this "joie de vivre." She said, "Il faut se faire plaisir tous les jours" – treat yourself or do something for yourself that makes you happy every single day. Forget anything that may be bothering you and take some time for yourself.

| 131) | Make French friends. |

It is not always easy to get to know your neighbors, especially in large cities where everyone seems to be busy with work or school or taking care of a family or their daily activities. But just like everywhere else, there are opportunities to get to know the people who live near you. If you come across a neighbor and they recognize you as their neighbor, they will most likely say hello to you out of politeness. Sometimes you will find that you have something in common with your neighbor and you may start up a conversation because perhaps you are both students or you are both parents or you like the same sports. I found that it takes a while to develop a friendship, but when you have a friend, they will be a friend for many years and maybe even life.

If you work, you will have opportunities to get to know your colleagues, and if you are a student, you will be in classes or activities with other students. Knowing French will help you find new friends and having friends will help you know and learn French. The only real way to learn a language and to have a complete understanding of our similarities and our differences is to make friends and to communicate as much as possible with them.

My old French teacher years ago told me that French was just like English. I didn't understand until I had lived for many years in France and could actually talk with other people on all types of topics. After a while, this foreign language will no longer be foreign to you.

Learning another language is a wonderful experience. It reminds me of a scene from a movie called "The Thirteenth Warrior" and how a character slowly absorbed the language and culture around him. The story takes place back in the times of the Vikings and Norsemen, and twelve Vikings are called upon to eliminate a monster that was destroying villages. The thirteenth warrior turned out to be an Arabian man, an "ambassador" from Baghdad (played by Antonio Banderas), who did not even speak

their language and had no knowledge of their culture. As
time passed, the Arabian man listened and observed and
one day, to the surprise of the Viking warriors,
understood what they all had said and spoke out to them
in their language. The beauty of the film stemmed from
the fact that you, the spectator, heard the Vikings
speaking their language, which was still a foreign
language and incomprehensible at the beginning of the
film, and then when the foreign ambassador finally
understood what they were saying, the film switched to
one language and they were speaking English and you
could understand everything they were saying, just like
the Arabian man.

This is exactly what happens when you make the
language your own. You no longer see people speaking
some foreign language. It becomes a language that you
understand. It becomes your own personal tool, your own
other language. Consequently, you no longer see these
other people as foreigners. You see them as people like
yourself and for some of them, as your friends.
Félicitations. You are on your way to seeing the world in
a different light. This is the new you, thanks to your life
in Paris.

Go on a virtual visit to Paris. Read my suggestions and check out pictures online that go with each suggestion. This list gives you what topic or topics to Google for each of my 131 ways to make your Parisian life easier:

1)	the Sorbonne, www.amazon.com/author/mariannely
2)	Paris cafés
3)	French fashion
4)	French coffee
5)	Parisian family
6)	Meeting Parisian friends in a café
7)	European table etiquette
8)	Images for a traversin, Foyer International des Etudiantes
9)	Parisian bakery picture
10)	Images for euros, images for currency exchange bureau Paris
11)	Images for French banks
12)	Images for ATM machines Paris
13)	Bûche de Noël, galette des rois, poisson d'avil, le muguet, Bastille Day, Halloween in Paris, All Saints Day Paris, New Year's Paris

14)	French calendar
15)	Paris pastry shop pictures, Paris charcuterie pictures
16)	Images for French individualism
17)	French houses in Paris pictures
18)	Flowers as gifts in pictures Paris
19)	Prix fixe menu
20)	French menus pictures, le cidre, citron préssé
21)	Les Français à table (French people at a dinner table), Club Med pictures
22)	Pictures of Paris during general strikes, traffic jams in Paris pictures
23)	Stick shift driving pictures, French driver's license pictures, clamps on car tires in Paris, Parisian cars parked on sidewalks, le métro Pris pictures, Paris buses, RER train Paris pictures
4)	Le code de la route pictures, priorité à droite pictures, le périphérique pictures, driving around the Arch of Triumph pictures
25)	Parisian cab driver pictures, speed limit in Paris pictures
26)	Picture carte de séjour, picture carte de résident Paris, picture Préfecture de Paris

27)	Pictures French euros, pictures marchés de Paris, typical Parisian apartment pictures, pictures small kitchens in Paris
28)	Picture washing machine in French kitchen
29)	Pictures rainy Paris, pictures Paris Plage
30)	Pictures shower facilities Paris, bidet in France pictures, gant de toilette picture
31)	Faire les bises pictures
32)	French breakfast pictures, French coffee bowl pictures, les baguettes et les tartines pictures, chausson aux pommes pictures, pain au chocolat pictures, images for French biscotte
33)	Le canard enchaîné pictures, Charlie Hebdo pictures, Louis de Funès pictures, Astérix et Obélix : Mission Cléopatre, La chèvre film, Bienvenue chez les Ch'tis pictures
34)	Popular French movies photos
35)	French wine pictures, French mineral water photos
36)	Passengers in the Paris métro photos
37)	Pictures étages d'immeubles Paris
38)	Pictures chambre de bonne Paris, pictures elevators Paris, Hotel le Royal Monceau

39)	Apartments in Paris photos
40)	Paris haute cuisine pictures
41)	Pictures le goûter Paris
42)	Dinnertime pictures Paris
43)	Pictures gas stations Paris, picture map of Paris métro
44)	Turkish toilets Paris
45)	Portes blindées pictures Paris
46)	Paris popular sports pictures, l'escrime pictures, Paris judo pictures, Roland-Garros pictures, le Tiercé pictures
47)	rue Saint-Denis, picture of map of Paris arrondissements, Paris Chinatown pictures
48)	French escargot pictures, French frog's legs, tripes, langue de boeuf, images for steak tartare
49)	Images for boucheries Paris, images for poissonnerie Paris, images for charcuterie Paris, images for crémerie Paris, images for fleuristes Paris
50)	French grocery bags pictures, un cabas à roulettes pictures, images for l'épicerie Paris
51)	Auchan, Monoprix, Casino

52)	Alcohol in Paris
53)	Naked statues Paris, images for Moulin Rouge, images for Lido
54)	French understatement cartoons
55)	French hand gesture pictures
56)	Lady toilet attendants Paris pictures, Jardin du Luxembourg chairs pictures
57)	Images for je n'ai plus faim, images for salle de bains
58)	Les Champs-Elysées, Arch of Triumph Paris, Concorde Square Paris, l'Opéra Paris pictures, Montmartre pictures, boulevard St. Michel pictures, Tour Montparnasse Paris pictures, images for la Grande Arche de la Défense, images for French cut park trees
59)	CRS Paris
60)	Images for French compliments
61)	L'officiel des spectacles, Pariscope, images for French movie theaters Paris, images for les ouveuses de cinéma
62)	Images for Ramadan in Paris, images for Chinatown in Paris, images for Russian community in Paris
63)	Images for standing in line in Paris

64)	Images for how French people slice apples
65)	Images for café waiters in Paris
66)	Images for dogs sitting in cafés in Paris
67)	Images for Paris electric outlets
68)	Images for boutique vêtements Paris
69)	Images for concierge d'immeubles Paris
70)	Images for pharmacies in Paris
71)	Images for hospitals in Paris
72)	Images for quiet Paris in August
73)	Images for sports d'hiver
74)	French school schedule example
75)	Images for la classe de mer, images for la classe poney, images for la classe de ski
76)	Images for le bac
77)	Images for le système scolaire en France
78)	Images for le treizième mois
79)	Images of dentists Paris
80)	Images for une maison de campagne

81)	Images palace of Versailles, images St. Germain-en-Laye, Disneyland Paris
82)	Images for l'assistante maternelle
83)	Images for la SNCF
84)	Images crêperies Paris
85)	Images for French clothing closets
86)	Images for pelouse interdite Paris
87)	Images for escalators in Paris métro
88)	Images for Parisian clothing price tags
89)	French individualism
90)	Images for Parisian open markets
91)	Images of French eating pizza with fork and knife
92)	Images of Parisian stores
93)	Images of French cheese with names
94)	Images for French yogurt
95)	Images for Parisian tourist sites
96)	Images of Parisian apartment buildings
97)	Images for inscriptions universitaires Paris

98)	Images for Parisian courtyards
99)	French political parties
100)	Images for French pastry, tarte tatin recipe, popular French cookies
101)	Images of shutters in Paris
102)	Images of checks with service compris
103)	RER train Paris pictures
104)	Images for Paris Vincennes Zoo
105)	Images for Monoprix
106)	Images of French mineral water
107)	Images for French perfume, Guerlain Champs-Elysées store
108)	Images for cold café drinks Paris
109)	Images for croque monsieur, images for croque madame
110)	Images for time zones in world
111)	Images for clunky hotel keys Paris
112)	Images for bed and breakfast Paris
113)	Images for Des racines et des ailes, images for Envoyé spécial

114)	Images for Paris catacombs, images for Paris sewers, images for Père Lachaise, images for son et lumière
115)	Images for U.S. consulate Paris
116)	Images of Parisian commuters reading
117)	Images of Charles de Gaulle Airport, images of Orly Airport
118)	Carte de visite personnelle
119)	Images for Minitel, images Cité des Sciences et de l'Industrie Porte de la Villette, images for French keyboard
120)	Image of street statues Paris
121)	Images for the Arch of Triumph, images for the Louvre, images for Versailles, images for the Eiffel Tower
122)	Images for French classic literature, images for la FNAC
123)	Tintin, Astérix
124)	Pictures French classrooms in Paris
125)	Classic French singers, Jean-Michel Jarre, Youtube ne me quitte pas, Youtube Hugues Aufray Santiago, youtube Jean-Michel Jarre Oxygène Live in Your Living Room

126)	Chocolate in Paris, Calissons d'Aix, French candy
127)	French ice cream cones
128)	Comité d'entreprise
129)	Images of a new you
130)	Images for happy Parisians
131)	Images for making friends through learning language

Printed in Great Britain
by Amazon